DETROIT'S
BIRWOOD WALL

DETROIT'S
BIRWOOD WALL

Hatred & Healing in the West Eight Mile Community

GERALD VAN DUSEN

Foreword by Reverend Jim Holley, PhD

THE
History
PRESS

Published by The History Press
Charleston, SC
www.historypress.com

First published 2019

Manufactured in the United States

ISBN 9781467142014

Library of Congress Control Number: 2019935342

CONTENTS

FOREWORD

Detroit is an iconic American city with a rich and storied past. When the final history of Detroit is written, whole chapters will be devoted to how the "Motor City" put the nation on wheels and how the "Arsenal of Democracy" helped win World War II. Yet another chapter will explore the city's rich musical heritage, including its contribution to twentieth-century popular music as the home of the "Motown Sound."

If the history is to be comprehensive, it must include certain darker realities as well. Rioting at the Sojourner Truth Housing Project in 1942 on the city's northeast side, on the Belle Isle Bridge in 1943 and on Twelfth Street in 1967 reveal the depth of racial discrimination woven into the fabric of life for many residents of Detroit.

And, of course, there will be a chapter on Detroit filing for Chapter 9 bankruptcy in 2013, the largest such municipal filing in U.S. history both by debt ($18 billion to $20 billion) and by population (700,000-plus).

One chapter that needs to be included in any comprehensive account of Detroit would be the story of a small community in northwest Detroit that fought to overcome an egregious series of barriers, most dramatically symbolized by the infamous "Birwood Wall," constructed in 1941 to even further isolate them from white Detroit.

The present volume, written ably and compassionately by Gerald Van Dusen, reveals perhaps for the first time how this isolated enclave of early settlers along Eight Mile Road chose the path of constructive engagement in the face of discrimination rather than the path of rioting and destruction.

Their story of overcoming obstacles is not over, for new and insidious barriers continue to be erected (think car insurance, banking and real estate redlining, as well as low broadband competition and deployment within communities of color and so forth).

Van Dusen's book will make you think. And maybe it will help each of us step out of our tightly circumscribed localities and confront the bigger world.

REVEREND JIM HOLLEY, PhD
Senior Pastor
The Historic Little Rock Baptist Church
Detroit, Michigan

PREFACE

I learned of the Wall when I was sixteen years old. Although I grew up on the far west side of Detroit, I attended an all-boys parochial high school located on Seven Mile Road on Detroit's northwest side. One day, a friend and classmate invited me to his house after school to work together on Latin and geometry homework. His house on Pinehurst was just a city block south of Eight Mile Road. After we finished our homework, we walked the neighborhood, and when we came across this long monolith of concrete on Mendota Street, my friend challenged me to scale the wall and walk its length—without falling. I followed his lead, although I was not as adept as him negotiating obstacles such as overhanging tree branches and tall shrubs abutting the Wall. As we walked slowly, he informed me that he had walked atop the Wall several times, as it was a sort of neighborhood initiation. Kids had actually injured themselves falling and landing awkwardly. As luck would have it, just before we reached Norfolk, the first completed section of the Wall, I stumbled over a tree branch, fell into a backyard of soft grass and lay unhurt.

I recall asking my friend, "Why exactly would anyone go to the time and expense of erecting such a formidable barrier to separate one neighborhood from another? Why not a simple chain link fence?" My friend simply replied, "It was built to keep people like me away from people like you." I don't remember anything else from that conversation or from that day, but I've never forgotten my friend's words.

A few years later, during the sweltering summer of 1967, I worked at a bank branch located in Detroit's inner city. In late July, black residents of Twelfth Street rebelled openly and violently against pervasive police harassment and neighborhood neglect by city hall, leading to the most horrific weeklong loss of life and destruction of property in the city's history. Kathryn Bigelow's evocative film *Detroit* chronicled but one aspect of the police brutality of the period. My bank manager notified each of us that it was business as usual, so we opened at 10:00 a.m. each morning of that week so that customers would have access to their accounts in those trying summer days. Customer after customer expressed the view that the violence and destruction of that week were "only a matter of time." Overcrowding caused by an urban renewal policy that wiped out the large segregated neighborhoods of Detroit's lower east side, "Black Bottom," coupled by police harassment by a largely white police force that targeted young black males, had come home to roost.

I immediately thought of the various efforts to isolate and denigrate the black residents east of the Wall along Eight Mile Road, and I wondered how and why that section of the city escaped similar violence and rebellion. I had studied both the Sojourner Truth Riot of 1942 on the northeast side and the 1943 riot downtown in my Social Psychology class in college. But there was no mention in any of my texts or in any class discussion of the Birwood Wall or the community that the Wall was intended to isolate.

This book describes how the residents of a one-square-mile area of northwest Detroit adapted to life in relative isolation from the more affluent, white neighborhoods encircling them. The Birwood Wall, constructed in 1941 to satisfy the Federal Housing Authority's requirement that the proposed new subdivision of middle-class homes not directly abut the principally black and substandard homes east of the Wall, seemed the perfect solution to both federal authorities and local real estate developers. Never considered in the equation was the effect the Wall would have on the black community, which for years had tried and failed to obtain financing of its own for standard housing construction. Residents continued to adapt, without violence, to the world around them, assisting one another in constructing makeshift abodes as well as supporting black-owned businesses, volunteering their time at the local, segregated schools and worshiping in the many exclusively black churches that had sprung up in the community.

Stepping outside the community was always a challenge, and the various barriers erected to exclude African Americans from equal access to essential city services, not to mention participation in Detroit's rich cultural life, only made them appreciate the support and sense of community they enjoyed upon returning home. The two riots that would occur in other parts of the city in successive years would serve to underscore the resilience of the West Eight Mile community. They were determined to work within the system to effect changes that would preserve and protect the community they loved. For nearly one hundred years, they have scaled every barrier designed to frustrate their progress.

ACKNOWLEDGEMENTS

I would like to express my gratitude to several individuals and organizations that furnished photographs and other primary sources of information.

Dwight Smith, president of the 8 Mile Old Timers' Club, was instrumental in providing me with photos and documents and helping me resolve conflicting sources of information. Night or day, Mr. Smith was always available to help me connect the dots.

I would always like to thank Teresa Moon, president of the 8 Mile Homeowners' Association, not only for her support and encouragement throughout the project but also for the connections she helped me establish with local residents and business owners, past and present, whose stories and recollections greatly enriched the narrative.

A few interviewees deserve special mention. Sophia Holley Ellis, ninety-two at the time of the interview, shared numerous stories about and insights into growing up as a child in the West Eight Mile enclave before she moved to Ann Arbor in pursuit of undergraduate and graduate degrees in biology and German at the University of Michigan in Ann Arbor. Gloria Butler provided priceless information about Royal Oak Township and Carver Elementary School. Marion Baxter described several instances of racial discrimination in downtown Detroit and at Lincoln High School in Ferndale.

For additional assistance in obtaining primary documents and historical photos, I would like to thank Marlena Tungstal of Oak Grove AME Church; Stevetta Johnson of Our Lady of Victory; Elizabeth Clemens of Wayne State University's Reuther Library; Carla Reczek of the Detroit

Public Library's Burton Historical Collection; Lisa Valerio-Nowc, library administrator, Charter Township of Royal Oak Public Library; Mike Wells Jr.; Kenneth Wells; Sophia Holley Ellis; Gloria Butler; Millicent Holley; Lauren Gohl; and Jan Froggatt, Roger Schmidt and Jean Spang of the Ferndale Historical Society.

Finally, I would like to thank John Rodrigue, acquisitions editor at The History Press, for seeing the important historical merit of the Birwood Wall project and believing that I could be the one to tell its story.

INTRODUCTION

The past is never dead. It's not even past.
—William Faulkner, Requiem for a Nun

The morning of August 3, 1941, was oppressively hot. A construction crew working for a local real estate developer in northwest Detroit arrived in an assortment of commercial vehicles, including flatbed trucks with trailers carrying diesel excavators and other heavy-duty equipment. The first order of business was to dig a trench, beginning 120 feet from the sidewalk fronting Eight Mile Road. As the excavator moved south, its bucket biting into the rocky soil just deep enough to penetrate the frost line, a cement footing was poured.

Work on the trench continued along the utility easement located in the alleyway between Mendota and Birwood Streets. The morning passed quickly, and children from as far away as Wyoming, four streets away, were drawn to the sights and sounds of the heavy-duty construction equipment. Something big was happening before their eyes, but no one knew what to make of it; even parents of the children who approached the construction site in the early evening hours, long after the project manager had left for the day, gaped in wonderment.

The work on the wall would continue for several days as the excavator reached Norfolk, the first cross street intersecting both Mendota and Birwood. The trench work picked up again across Norfolk and moved southward to Chippewa. The final segment of footings began on the other side of Chippewa and extended all the way to 7½ Mile Road, which had been renamed Pembroke. Once all the footings had cured, the construction crew began erecting a wall, made of concrete blocks, six feet tall and one foot thick. The wall would run for half a mile, with interruptions for vehicular traffic at Norfolk and Chippewa.

INTRODUCTION

Although no one on the Birwood Street side quite knew what to make of the wall at the time, its purpose would be revealed in the days following. The wall had been created as a barrier between the community east of the wall, predominantly African American, and a new real estate development being built for an exclusively white clientele just west of the wall.

The real estate developer had approached the FHA with plans to develop the property west of Birwood the previous year, only to have his application rejected because the proposed project bordered directly on a "hazardous" neighborhood, as defined by Home Owners' Loan Corporation's City Survey Program. The FHA was reluctant to insure bank loans on such properties because racially mixed areas, the agency reasoned, were likely to stir confrontation, lead to violence and jeopardize the fiscal soundness of the investment. Undaunted, the developer approached the FHA a second time with a new proposal: he would construct a wall, six feet high and one foot thick, between the "hazardous" neighborhood east of Mendota and the proposed new development. The FHA agreed to the compromise.

A view of the Birwood Wall, August 1941, constructed to separate an existing settlement of African American homeowners and a new development of homes sold exclusively to whites. *Library of Congress.*

Behind the scenes, the Carver Progressive Club, founded and registered with the State of Michigan in 1940 as a neighborhood improvement organization, attempted to halt construction of the wall by making inquiries of its own and by confronting the developer. The club had set up a committee to investigate the purpose behind its construction and, hopefully, dissuade the developer from completing the project.

At a meeting called to discuss the committee findings, the committee spokesperson said, "We talked with the man who is head of the developing company. He said the wall is on his property and there wasn't anything we could do about it. He further said that he was forced to shut off the view of our dilapidated houses to increase his chances of selling those homes on Mendota. Those homes are FHA approved too."[1]

And so the wall, built exactly as it was proposed to the FHA, was completed in August 1941. Members of the Carver Progressive Club were disheartened but not so discouraged to give up their fight to improve housing conditions within the community.

THE GREAT MIGRATION

Between 1910 and 1950, many roads led to Detroit. Migrants came from the East and from the South—especially the South—to claim jobs offered by zealous factory recruiters, posted daily on factory billboards and advertised in newspaper classifieds. Factories and suppliers were trying to compete with Henry Ford's offer of "five dollars a day" for assemblers in his automobile factory and were having a hard time filling all the positions through much of the period before the beginning of the First World War and immediately after the Second World War.

This northern port city was already known to many African Americans in the South for the critical role it played in discreetly assisting runaway slaves escape across its namesake river to freedom in Canada. Migrating north through treacherous terrain, fugitive slaves sought to reach "Midnight," the code name for Detroit, as the final stop on the Underground Railroad. Those who made it found respite at the "Croghan Street Station," code name for the basement of the Second Baptist Church, one of the oldest black churches in the Midwest. Now, half a century after the Emancipation Proclamation, blacks were arriving in Detroit to flee Jim Crow and find economic opportunity.

In April 1918 Cornelia Davis moved with her family from upstate New York to Detroit seeking a better way of life.[2] At nearly the same time, Antonio Rosa and Mary Gillem arrived from Piqua, Ohio, where they had been refused a marriage ceremony because they were an interracial couple.[3] Both families managed to bypass the major settlement of working-class black families in Detroit's crowded lower east side and settled instead on unincorporated land eight miles north of city center. Mary Gillem's twin brothers, James and Luke, had settled there months before and were anxious for Antonio and Mary to join them. What Cornelia Davis, Antonio Rosa and Mary Gillem found upon their arrival was a sparsely populated community with few finished homes, some tar-papered houses, tents, farms and lean-to dwellings scattered among trees, muddy roads, ditches and paths. There were a few stores and restaurants on both sides of Eight Mile but not much else.

John Crews, on the other hand, knew nothing of the Eight Mile Road enclave when he arrived in Detroit the very same year as the Davis family and Antonio Rosa and Mary Gillem were settling in.[4] For most working-class blacks who arrived in Detroit for work, the lower east side appeared to be the only residential option.

The Detroit of 1918 was both large and populous. Founded in 1701 as a French colony, Fort Pontchartrain du Detroit was mainly a trading post for the exchange of furs from Native Americans who had settled within the area and French settlers with goods supplied by traders from Montreal. Having changed hands with the British by the Treaty of Paris in 1763, the settlement formally became known as Detroit. In 1806, 770 residents shared an area of just 0.33 square mile. Owing to substantial immigration from Eastern and Central Europe, annexation of adjacent land barely kept pace with the city's growing population. By 1918, the city of Detroit would occupy 77.31 square miles of land to accommodate nearly 1 million residents, including more than 40,000 African Americans who had migrated north.[5]

Life for the Crews family would prove less of an adventure and more of a struggle to survive the vicissitudes of urban life. It was certainly a far cry from tenant farming in rural Barbour County, Alabama, or coal mining in Little Logan, West Virginia. But they had made these dramatic adjustments before, and they were prepared for the hardships that lie ahead.[6]

John had arrived first in Detroit with the intent of finding employment and obtaining accommodations for his family. He quickly secured employment with American Car and Foundry, which had previously manufactured train cars but now, during World War I, converted to war production. Jobs requiring physical labor were readily available, he quickly learned, but adequate accommodations were less easy to find. Finally, after many local inquiries and consultation with the Detroit Urban League, a new

Second Baptist Church, on Detroit's lower east side, functioned as a station on the Underground Railroad, providing sanctuary for fugitive slaves. *Author's collection.*

Right: State historical marker commemorating the site of the oldest African American church in the Midwest. *Author's collection.*

Below: Sculpture commemorating Detroit's role in the Underground Railroad. Located in Hart Plaza on the Detroit River, the sculpture depicts six fugitive slaves ready to board a barge to freedom across the river in Windsor, Ontario. *Author's collection.*

organization created to help people like himself, he had arranged, if only temporarily, to share the upstairs rear portion of a four-family flat with the Thisteltons at 1926 Russell Street on the lower east side of Detroit, an area known as Black Bottom. Very soon he was able to send Lizzie sufficient funds for two one-way train tickets to Detroit.

John was pleased that the train carrying his wife, Lizzie, and daughter, Burneice, was not due to arrive until after 6:00 pm, so he would not have to ask his employer to leave early. Employees at the foundry had already been criticized by management—with pointed reference to the "Negro" employees—for missing too many days of work, particularly after payday. The steady job meant too much to John to risk the wrath of his new boss.

Michigan Central Depot was a beehive of activity, with more than two hundred trains per day arriving and departing.[7] Once he was able to locate the right track, John flagged down Lizzie and Burneice, who were so happy to be reunited. Outside the depot, along Michigan Avenue, the Crewses were able to catch a taxi that took them across Woodward, still without electrified traffic signals, into Detroit's lower east side and onto Russell Street, a neighborhood teeming with crowded sidewalks and Jewish shops.

The new accommodations were cramped but workable when everyone was courteous and shared the work of keeping the flat neat and orderly. Adding to Lizzie's frustration, however, was the constant reminder that nearly all the furniture in the flat belonged to the Thistletons and needed to be respected, with the clear implication that perhaps Burneice should spend more time in the bedroom and less time on the furniture in the parlor.

Realizing the strain the Thistletons were putting on his family, John began to look elsewhere in the neighborhood for more permanent and more spacious accommodations. On his way home from work one day, John noticed a coal truck being loaded with furniture just down the street from their flat. After inquiring from the truck driver of the whereabouts of the landlord, he was able to reach the rental agent and subsequently arranged to rent the entire downstairs flat at 2019 Russell Street.

THE CREWSES WERE HARDLY alone in their search for affordable housing within the city limits. Before the First World War, blacks in Detroit, numbering nearly 5,000, constituted less than 1 percent of the city's total population, and these individuals were relatively easily absorbed within the area's various ethnic neighborhoods. As the great migration of rural southerners took hold, competition for good jobs and desirable housing pitted white against

Exterior view of Michigan Central Depot, September 10, 1980. *Walter P. Reuther Library, Archives of Labor and Urban Affairs, Wayne State University.*

black. By 1920, Detroit's black population well surpassed 40,000 in a city of nearly 1 million, and white ethnic neighborhoods, composed increasingly of southern whites, were less inclined to welcome this large influx of southern blacks.[8]

Whatever difficulties they may have had in finding adequate housing in Detroit, African Americans had a double motive for abandoning the South. The plantation economy of the South—so dependent on sharecropping and tenant farming—offered little opportunity to advance beyond bare subsistence. Increased mechanization of farming, as well as the destructive impact of the boll weevil epidemic, created a labor oversupply, and what farm work was available now favored unemployed whites.

In addition to economics, blacks continued to suffer from ongoing forms of terrorism in the white supremacist "Jim Crow" South. Although the KKK had technically been disbanded in 1869, it merely went underground. Violence against persons and property continued as tools of intimidation and social control. Voting rights were routinely suppressed through the imposition of poll taxes and literacy tests. The court system offered little relief from injustice, particularly involving racial disputes. And the bifurcated southern educational system ("separate but equal") left black children with

Child labor on tenant farm, Ellis County, Texas. *Library of Congress.*

overcrowded classrooms and a shortage of textbooks, desks, blackboards and basic supplies, as well as with overworked, underpaid and often poorly trained teachers.[9]

Still, leaving the South was a difficult and courageous act, and many blacks who trekked north found work in large cities such as Mobile and Montgomery, Alabama, or Atlanta, Georgia, without ever having to cross the Mason-Dixon line. In fact, had relentless spring rains and melting mountain snow not burst the local dam, leading to a cave-in at the Little Eagle Mining Company, the Crewses may have built a life in Logan County, West Virginia, and never made it any farther north.

Tenant farm on cotton lands of Ellis County, Texas. *Library of Congress.*

Drinking fountain on the county courthouse lawn, Halifax, North Carolina. *Library of Congress.*

BLACK BOTTOM AND PARADISE VALLEY

Even on the near east side of Detroit, where the majority of African Americans were steered at their arrival, the accommodations John Crews found on Russell Street, at first and then again weeks later, was fortuitous. In the months and years to follow, the Crewses, like so many of their African American brethren who had escaped from southern oppression, would experience great difficulty finding housing that was neither substandard nor in need of major repair. Segregation had forced a growing number of black migrants to Detroit into the older, more dilapidated and overcrowded sections of the city, and city services like garbage collection and housing inspections were spotty. Add to this health concerns such as epidemics of tuberculosis, scarlet fever and influenza, which struck this community harder than any other area of the city. Despite these squalid conditions, blacks had few other choices and had also to bear the brunt of unscrupulous landlords who knew the demand was so great they could ignore requests for desperately needed repairs to these flats and apartments and still charge exorbitant rent.[10]

Inevitably, the Crewses' landlord came calling not only to collect the monthly rent but to announce a ten-dollar increase beginning the following month. This was on top of the increase just the month before. Black renters like the Crewses had few options other than to search elsewhere for accommodations, which was becoming increasingly difficult; accept the rent increase, albeit begrudgingly; or sign a land contract with an owner or agent of the same or other property at a fixed interest for a specified period. On the surface, this third option seemed to have many benefits for the purchaser: the contract would eliminate the unreasonable increases in rent; the new owner would acquire equity in a property; and the new owner could, and was often encouraged to, make property improvements and repairs without having to wait for a recalcitrant landlord. The devil, the Crewses would soon learn, was in the details.

The Crewses knew that these unrestrained rent increases would inevitably drive them off Russell Street. With little money to purchase a property, they knew their options were limited. However, a "fixer upper" on nearby Lumpkin Street came on the market, and the real estate agent seemed amenable to offering land contract terms. The Crewses jumped at the opportunity to own a two-story property, despite having no bathroom on either floor but having an outside toilet situated on the rear of the lot. So long as he enjoyed steady, full-time employment, John Crews believed

African American residence near Hastings Street in Black Bottom section of Detroit. *Library of Congress.*

he could keep up with the high monthly payments; at least the days of rent gouging were over. Lizzie could now invite her sister Ada to Detroit from Kentucky.

In the wake of massive overcrowding on Detroit's near east side, the Jewish community that had originally settled the Hastings Street area was now gradually relocating to an area around Oakman Boulevard on the west side of Woodward Avenue and then on to Twelfth Street and Dexter in its slow, almost generational exodus to northwest Detroit. Having no similar options available, African Americans swallowed up the vacated properties the moment they became available. Residual Jewish businesses continued

African American residence in Black Bottom, Detroit. *Library of Congress.*

to operate in Paradise Valley, Black Bottom's predominant business district and entertainment center.[11]

Before long, Lizzie's sister Ada moved to Detroit, settling in long enough to meet, marry and move out of the overcrowded ghetto that Black Bottom had become. Ada and her new husband, Marshall, purchased a small plot in a new subdivision just outside the city between Wyoming and Livernois Avenues and south of Eight Mile. The city of Detroit's fairly regular and rapid annexation of land had not yet extended to Eight Mile Road. The subdivision, now being called Garden Homes Subdivision, was one of the few areas anywhere near Detroit that was open for sale to African Americans, and lots were selling briskly. Precious few whites had settled in this area of unannexed land, and the many blacks who did were beginning to form a community of like-minded pioneers.

The land at issue was part of a much larger parcel owned by Henry G. Stevens, a Detroit philanthropist and first president of the Detroit Urban League, an organization founded on principles of racial harmony, if not full integration. Stevens would sell the land to real estate developers intent on breaking the parcel up into small, affordable lots.[12] Once purchased, it was hoped, construction would begin on housing that would absorb some of the pressure overcrowding and blight were creating on Detroit's near east side. The Interurban streetcar line serviced the new area of development, so transportation for employment to and from the city did not seem to be the issue. The only other working-class community of color was the village of Inkster to the west of Detroit, where many black Ford factory workers, rejected by the close-in suburb of Dearborn, discovered they could live without threat of violence or intimidation.

Back in the city, the Crewses were struggling with the unforgiving terms of a high-interest land contract. It was bad enough that the original sale price had been badly inflated, but the frustration with having to address the nagging structural, electrical and plumbing repairs was surpassed only by the indignity of relying on a backyard toilet. When the inevitable day came during the postwar depression that he was laid off at the foundry, John was almost relieved. The strain of life on Lumpkin Street was palpable. And so, when the inevitable eviction letter arrived, notifying the Crewses that their single missed payment triggered the repossession clause that lay deep within the legalese of their contract, they knew it was time for a radical change in their lives.

THE MOVE TO EIGHT MILE ROAD

Change came for the Crewses in the form of an invitation by Ada and Marshall to stay with them in the Eight Mile subdivision. Since the subdivision had not yet been annexed by the city, there was no municipal water service available. The nearest source of clean water was a quarter mile away. Yet the growing community of black settlers was making do, perhaps a residual capacity left over from adapting to life in the agrarian South. The Interurban provided service beyond the city limits and made a stop at Eight Mile, although the stop was nearly a mile from the subdivision. John could catch the Interurban each morning to a new labor construction job he had landed, helping to build the offices for the Braun Lumber Company on Davison in the city.

The construction skills John Crews would acquire at Braun Lumber would stand him in good stead on Eight Mile Road. Carpentry skills were at a premium within the subdivision. Since banks charged private contractors who were willing to build in the area higher interest rates, few residents were able to afford these professional services. Instead, many residents built the main floor as a foundation and then set vertical poles in each corner to support what amounted to a large tent with walls made up of whatever malleable materials they could find. And still others constructed shacks, piece by piece, as lumber was purchased and scrap material became available locally.

Social workers dispatched to the area from the newly formed Detroit Urban League were distressed by the conditions under which residents lived their daily lives. With neither running water nor electricity, these migrants, it was feared, had "reverted" to their southern roots.[13] They were, in fact, simply recoiling from the unhealthy and inhospitable conditions within Black Bottom, where private space and good nutrition were at a premium. Here homeowners engaged in subsistence farming, decorative gardening and small livestock breeding, particularly of chickens, hogs and goats. Unpurchased lots became community gardens. If they were to be rejected in their efforts at integrating with Detroit's white majority, then they would need to become self-sufficient. The unannexed land on both sides of Eight Mile Road created an opportunity for blacks to reject the transient nature of life on Detroit's near east side and to develop a family-oriented community close enough to the big city for employment purposes but far enough away to avoid its inequities and iniquities.

COMMUNITIES OF FAITH WITHIN THE WEST EIGHT MILE ROAD COMMUNITY

Elizabeth Crews would busy herself helping Ada with domestic chores and getting Burneice situated at Lockport School. Never far from her mind, however, was filling a spiritual need. She would not have to go very far to find it. There were now several churches within walking distance of Eight Mile and Wyoming: Mount Beulah Baptist Church, Oak Grove, First Baptist (later New Prospect), Church of God in Christ, Calvary AME Zion, Hamlett Temple, St. Paul Methodist and Our Lady of Victory Catholic Church, which served both the Detroit side of Eight Mile as well as Royal Oak Township. Elizabeth would soon gravitate to the fledgling Oak Grove AME Church and become an integral part of its early development.

Part of the cohesiveness of the Eight Mile community can be traced to the efforts of a few of its earliest settlers to establish churches for community worship. Among the earliest endeavors was that of Cornelia Davis, who had come from New York, where she had been active in the AME Zion Church. Upon arrival at the Eight Mile enclave, she felt in her heart the desire to establish such a church, and her desire was soon shared by others already living nearby, including Anna Eaton Thomas, Princess Boyd and Lucille Smoot. A neighborhood resident, Mrs. Thompson, graciously lent her home to be used to organize a Sunday school for the local children. In the warm summer months, weather permitting, adults of the Methodist faith, under the leadership of Mrs. Davis, would assemble out of doors for a tent service. During the winter months, arrangements were made to use the Lockport School on Wisconsin Street. As there was a small Baptist congregation also seeking a temporary winter sanctuary, it was proposed and agreed on that the Methodists and Baptists would alternate their use of the facility, with the Baptists worshiping at Lockport one Sunday and the Methodists the following Sunday. They invited each other to join in their services and subsequently merged choirs and congregations so that a Sunday did not go by where a congregant could not give praise communally. The spirit of ecumenism filled Lockport School on Sundays, even as each congregation worked separately to raise money to construct its own church and retain its special identity.[14]

Over the next few years, a Women's Club, organized by Mrs. Davis, sponsored bazaars, ice cream socials and other affairs to raise money for the church. Originally organized as St. Luke African Methodist Episcopal Church, its name would soon be changed to Oak Grove, as it was learned

Mount Beulah Church, Detroit. *Author's collection.*

that an AME church named St. Luke already existed in Highland Park. A down payment from the funds held by the Women's Club secured a property at the corner of Chippewa and Kentucky, the site being chosen in deference to Mrs. Davis, who lived nearby.

In 1921, Nelson Smoot, a congregant and master carpenter, agreed to accept $60 to draw plans for the church and build it from used lumber that was obtained from the Gifford Lumber Company for just over $100. The lumber yard donated much of the millwork, such as window frames and so forth, to aid the small congregation. Since there was a chance that delivery trucks might get stuck in the loose sand that made up the streets leading to Oak Grove, Mr. Eldridge, a local man who had a team of horses, agreed to bring the lumber to the building site.

In 1924, disaster fell. The church caught fire and burned to the ground. Fortunately, a $2,000 insurance policy had been taken out at the time of original construction, and these funds helped with the process of rebuilding.

In Detroit's long and troubled history of race relations, Roman Catholic leadership, from the chancery on down to the parish, exercised the same degree of insensitivity to the needs of African Americans as other institutions. For much of the twentieth century, blacks were "discouraged," if not directly turned away at the vestibule of the dozens of ethnic neighborhood

Above: Oak Grove AME Church, Detroit. *Rogers Wm. Foster*.

Left: Cornerstone, Oak Grove AME Church, Detroit. *Author's collection*.

parishes. Before 1943, black Catholics in Detroit had few choices to worship communally on Sundays. Sacred Heart Church on Detroit's near east side was converted from a German to an African American parish in 1938. St. Benedict the Moor served black Catholics on Detroit's west side since 1927. And Holy Ghost parish, situated in the Seven Mile and Ryan area on the northeast side, was founded in 1939 to accommodate the many black Catholics who were refused entry to local churches west of Woodward.[15]

Anna Bates arrived in the United States from Trinidad at the age of seventeen and settled in Royal Oak Township around 1920. As a devout Catholic, Anna was disheartened to be turned away from the nearest Catholic church, Presentation, located on Meyers Road and Pembroke.[16] She began attending St. James, the next nearest, on Nine Mile and Woodward, a good five-mile walk completely outside the city of Detroit every Sunday morning. After bearing two children with her husband, Keith, Anna made up her mind to establish a Catholic mission close to home. She first contacted the nuns at Marygrove College on Six Mile Road to help her with the canonical process, and she also called the archdiocese, repeatedly, to request a priest to be assigned to the mission.

Essentially, a philosophical debate arose as a result of the inquiry with the archdiocese. From the perspective of the chancery downtown, why send a priest to a newly formed mission when there were so few registered Catholics in the area? One report suggests there were fewer than ten Catholic families in the whole of the West Eight Mile community. From Anna Bates's perspective, the new African American enclave was ripe with opportunity to expand Catholic outreach in an otherwise Protestant community. Seeing so many children in the neighborhoods north and south of Eight Mile Road, Anna could not help but envision a time when they were called to God's grace through the intercession of the good nuns of Marygrove College.

Anna's persistence paid off, as Sheldon Johnson at Birdhurst agreed in 1943 to open up the recreation center for a summer school program for children under the tutelage of the IHM sisters of Marygrove. The program proved a great success, and just two years later, more than three hundred children were enrolled in the sessions. At the same time the children's spiritual needs were being met, Archbishop Edward Mooney finally responded to Anna's call for a priest to formally open a mission for the West Eight Mile community. Anna had already made arrangements to lease a small storefront on Eight Mile and Cherrylawn, in consultation with Monsignor John Ryan, director of the Confraternity of Christian Doctrine of the Archdiocese of Detroit. All that was needed now was a priest to christen "Our Lady of Victory." Father

Alvin Deem, a Franciscan from nearby Duns Scotus College in Southfield, volunteered for the project. Seminarians and brothers from the college did repairs on the property and gave it a fresh coat of paint in preparation for the mission's first mass on October 3, 1943.

Thomas "Doc" Washington, owner of a number of businesses in the area, was so impressed with what Anna Bates—now addressed locally as "Mother" or "Madre" Bates—and Father Deem had accomplished within the community in such a short time that he decided to donate a parcel of land on the corner of Eight Mile and Washburn for a new church. By the end of World War II, the little storefront mission had grown considerably, such that a new, larger facility was urgently needed. And so, a basement was dug out and a foundation was laid on the donated land on Eight Mile and Washburn. An old long-closed east side church, St. Juliana's, was purchased, moved and set on the newly poured foundation. On December 15, 1946, Cardinal Edward Mooney offered prayers and formal dedication.[17]

The school building fund was growing steadily, so much so that by 1954 groundbreaking plans could be scheduled. The fifth black parish in the history of the Archdiocese of Detroit now had a school, and it would be the first Catholic school in Detroit to offer kindergarten. Father Deem had invited the Oblate Sister of Providence to provide for the educational needs of the West Eight Mile children. This historic black teaching order of nuns, whose mother house was centered in Baltimore, Maryland, graciously accepted the invitation and began arriving as early as 1948 to minister to local needs. As role models for black children—particularly impressionable young girls—in the neighborhoods, they were an ideal fit. Both the school and the church continued to grow and prosper for the next twenty years.

A sad ending came in 1975, when the archdiocese announced plans for a merger of Our Lady of Victory and Presentation Parishes owing to the steep decline in membership at Presentation following the wave of white flight to the suburbs. Ironically, the parish that had refused black participation a quarter century earlier was now opening its arms in acceptance. For the next seven years, parishioners remained in their own buildings as technical details—and politicking—were worked through. By 1982, the merger was complete, assets were sold off and Our Lady of Victory was no more.[18]

In Royal Oak Township, communities of faith flourished particularly in the 1940s and 1950s, with the phenomenal growth due in large part to the explosive population influx during the wartime years. By 1950, there were twenty-one churches in the township, with individual memberships running from about fifteen to three hundred. The church edifices ran from a single

Our Lady of Victory Catholic Church, Detroit. *Author's collection.*

room to a rather substantial structure with seating capacity of more than four hundred. Facilities for youth activities in all twenty-one churches were very limited or nonexistent. However, within the general religious program of most churches, some provision was made for Bible study, youth nights and vacation Bible school.[19]

Church membership was very mobile, as it was in the rest of the township, owing to the planned urban renewal that would eventually dislocate thousands of residents from their "temporary" wartime housing. In some churches, as high as 50 percent of the membership lived in surrounding communities. About 6 percent of the families in the township were Catholic and shared Our Lady of Victory Church with Detroit parishioners across

Eight Mile Road. Interestingly, information from Protestant churches in Detroit suggested that a significant percentage of their members were residents of the township and journeyed across the road to attend services.

The formal level of education of the clergy in these township churches was limited. Of the twenty-one churches, only one minister had a BD degree, and all the others had less than college training, with a high percentage with less than a high school diploma. However, 60 percent of the ministers with limited formal training had attended some Bible training school. Significantly, 70 percent of the ministers of the twenty-one churches lived outside the township.[20]

Financially, each church needed substantial financial assistance from its respective congregations. In fact, some of the churches were unable to go beyond the level of a basement in their building program during this period. With the exception of two of the churches in the township, the ministers were employed at an additional full-time job or seeking such employment because of the church's limited finances.

JOINING THE DETROIT PUBLIC SCHOOL SYSTEM

Lockport, the little red brick country school building with its two outside toilets and stove heat, was becoming inadequate for the children's day-to-day use. In the early 1920s, the local school board of Greenfield Township, serving the unannexed area just outside the jurisdiction of the Detroit system, made arrangements to have the children of Eight Mile attend Birdhurst School on Woodingham Drive to the east. White children from the surrounding area also attended Birdhurst, and for two years, all seemed to be going well. Apparently, the friendships being developed between the white and black children were becoming distasteful to many white parents. When the school closed for summer vacation in 1922, it would not reopen in the fall—the adjacent white school board made sure of that. For most of the black schoolchildren in the Eight Mile community, it would be back to Lockport. Some few parents were able to send their youngsters to schools in downtown Detroit and boarded them with local relatives.[21]

In the years following, Eight Mile Road took on the contours of a settled community. In 1924, however, frustration grew among some of its most outspoken inhabitants over the continued lack of water, lights and neighborhood schools—conditions that could be fixed if the area were annexed by the City of Detroit. To this end, a petition would need to be filed downtown, costing $1,200, which covered attorney and filing fees. Two families within the community declined signing the petition. To place the proposal on the ballot, 1,200 signatures from the citizens of Detroit would need to be obtained as well. In November, voters approved the annexation of the Eight Mile Road community, bounded by Eight Mile to the north, Greenlawn to the east, Wyoming to the West and Pembroke (renamed from 7½ Mile Road) to the south.[22]

In 1926, the City of Detroit annexed the Brightmoor area, farther west along Eight Mile Road. This would be the city's final annexation of land, owing to new legislation fashioned in Lansing curbing future annexations.

With annexation came the hope for modern facilities and an improved curriculum to educate the children of the Eight Mile community. However, the Detroit Public School System was under tremendous strain. During World War I, school construction had come to a virtual halt, despite dramatic increases in enrollment. From the end of the war in 1918 until 1935, the system experienced a growth rate of nearly 10 percent per year, growing from 95,023 in 1918 to 268,323 students in 1935. Thus, just to keep pace, the school system needed to construct facilities to accommodate at least 10,000 seats per year. In addition to the problems of determining construction locations and developing new curricula to serve specialized needs, the board had to first convince the voting public and municipal government to approve the increases and bond sales for all the planned projects. New communities under recent annexation, like the Eight Mile and Brightmoor communities, had to wait their turn.[23]

In 1925, the Detroit school board purchased a site on Pembroke, stretching from Northlawn to Roselawn Streets, on the southeastern edge of the community, thirteen blocks from Birwood. Pembroke remained the invisible barrier between the local black and white communities, and perhaps, as Burneice Avery was later to observe, the Detroit board was naïve enough to believe that the new school could serve both white and black communities.[24] A basement was dug, but the site was subsequently abandoned by the school district. A new site on the corner of Wisconsin and Chippewa Streets was purchased the following year. Located nearly in the exact center of the community, Higginbotham School, named after the architect who designed it, opened its first completed unit in the fall of 1927.

BLACK-OWNED BUSINESSES

Both before and after annexation, the community was well served by a black-owned commercial strip along Eight Mile Road. On the Detroit side, there was the Lett store, Worthy's, McCuller's Community Store, Charlie Rich's Pool Hall, Alfred Davis's Funeral Home and Thomas "Doc" Washington's drugstore. "Doc" also owned Uncle Tom's BBQ. There were white-owned businesses as well, including Jim Dolan's, an Atlantic & Pacific Supermarket in Royal Oak Township, Sim's Gas Station and Cockfield Funeral Home. Alice Newman recalled how her father, Jimmy Cain, managed several successful businesses on the north side of Eight Mile Road, including producing stage shows where he shared the stage as a musician.[25] Ms. Newman vividly recalled performing in his shows as a dancer, earning a quarter a week. Perhaps her clearest and most colorful memory, however, was the hot dog stand her father operated on Parkside and Eight Mile Road, called "Jimmy's," which became a popular hangout for young people. Hot dogs and soda pop were a nickel each, and a bowl of chili was a quarter. When her grandmother felt up to baking, single slices of her sweet potato pie sold out quickly. Local kids enjoyed the varieties of gum and candy available but especially loved playing the slot machine in the back, with its spinning lemons and oranges and other colorful fruit.

Considering that there were fewer than five hundred African American–owned businesses registered in the entire state of Michigan in 1929, West Eight Mile Road was a haven of black entrepreneurs.[26] During the early '30s, the black-owned businesses fronting Eight Mile Road were wiped out when the state highway department decided to widen the road. The local businesses tried but failed in court to stop the proposed project, and so another chapter of black entrepreneurship was lost to the annals of local history.

The widening of Eight Mile Road was a reflection of the city's population growth and mobility. With further annexation of land no longer an option, the housing crisis came into sharp relief. This crisis can hardly be overstated, as the Great Depression affected Detroit profoundly. So much of its economy depended on the auto industry, which employed about 10 percent, or 160,000, of the city's 1.6 million population. Variations of a favorite aphorism used in different parts of the country began making the rounds: "When the country catches a cold, Detroit catches pneumonia." As elsewhere, families within the West Eight Mile community were affected by job loss. Many lost their homes.

Left: Maude's Beauty Shop, Royal Oak Township, 1950s. *Dwight Smith*.

Right: Squall's Grocery Store, Royal Oak Township, 1950s. *Dwight Smith*.

On the national level, the election of Franklin D. Roosevelt in 1933 ushered in a series of "New Deal" programs and projects created in response to these dire economic conditions. Among the many agencies created were the Federal Housing Administration (FHA) and the Home Loan Bank Board. The FHA was designed to stabilize the housing market by providing insurance on loans tendered by the banking and loan industry. Similarly, under the supervision of the Federal Home Loan Bank Board (FHLBB), the Home Owners' Loan Corporation (HOLC) was authorized to provide new mortgages on an emergency basis to homeowners at risk of losing their homes due to foreclosure.

In 1935, HOLC began deviating from its original mission to assist homeowners avoid losing their homes to foreclosure and, for the next five years, developed a City Survey Program designed to assess risk levels for long-term real estate investment and to stabilize the appraising industry. HOLC agents traveled the country to gather data from local realtors and appraisers in more than two hundred cities. Particular neighborhoods within a city such as Detroit were graded thusly: A. Green: Best; B. Blue: Still Desirable; C. Yellow: Declining; and D. Red: Hazardous. Although the term "redlining" was not coined until the 1960s, it clearly applied in 1940 to neighborhoods with minority occupants, which were considered high risk for mortgage lenders. As one might expect, the Eight Mile–Wyoming neighborhood was graded "hazardous."[27]

Efforts to further isolate the community, under the guise of protecting property values, would soon surface. After the Second World War, with FHA guidelines changed (and restrictive covenants ruled unenforceable), single-family houses began to go up on both sides of the wall with deliberate speed. In 1946, a more comprehensive plan to "protect" white property values emerged in the Detroit City Planning Commission. This proposal suggested that the city maintain a green space buffer, twenty feet wide, around the Detroit perimeter of the community. Although the plan was never enacted, piecemeal efforts by a host of white actors managed to do just that. For example, Jewish real estate developer Harry Slatkin proposed, in 1953, extending the wall at Pembroke in a direction perpendicular to Birwood Street to further separate the African American community from his Jewish clientele to the south. He would promote the development as "one of northwest Detroit's last and most fashionable residential areas."[28] When the city building department rejected his permit request, he was undeterred. A six-foot-high solid wood fence, six blocks in length, was constructed along Pembroke, from Wyoming to Cherrylawn. Once again, efforts by the Carver Progressive Club to intercede on behalf of the Eight Mile community proved fruitless. When reached by phone to request a meeting, Slatkin purportedly replied, "East is east, and west is west and never the twain shall meet…at least not in our day. I see no reason or purpose in meeting with your committee."[29] Eventually, however, Slatkin's fence deteriorated to the point that it had to be removed. The Birwood Wall would stand for many more years.

The issue of race in Detroit remains complex and multifaceted. For the residents of the West Eight Mile Road community, a most unsettling question remained: how could the color of one's skin have elicited so visceral a response from other individuals, groups and institutions that a segregation wall was necessary to construct? It had not been necessary to construct a physical barrier such as this one for other despised groups, like the Jews, or other ethnic groups that had settled in areas of Detroit where they were not wanted. What specifically had they done? But the worst of it was not the wall. The wall on Birwood Street was just so many tons of cement. As a symbol, the wall embodies the many daily barriers that African Americans have had to overcome in order to survive. These societal barriers—what epidemiologists and community health officials call

Slatkin's fence, 1970. *Burton Historical Collection, Detroit Public Library.*

the social and economic determinants of health—include the conditions of one's housing, one's employment situation, access to transportation, quality of diet (including food insufficiency), level of education and other considerations. The daily lives of African Americans were directly affected by policies and actions taken by entities they had little understanding of and even less control over. How this group of urban settlers overcame these barriers is a tale worth the telling.

Chapter 1

THE CONTOURS OF THE ENCLAVE

B y the end of World War I, the community along Eight Mile Road, though small, had become well established. Its stability was based not on the number of families, the years in residence or even on the physical proximity of one neighbor to another; rather, it was based on the many relationships formed by common needs and interests. Joint activities—sharing homebuilding skills, establishing a local church, cultivating a garden, supporting local black-owned businesses, serving on school committees or simply celebrating the birth of a baby or a wedding—strengthened existing bonds and helped the community confront barriers placed in its path by external entities. In the coming years, various physical, legal and social barriers—the Birwood Wall, Slatkin's fence, restrictive covenants, segregated schools and lack of access to public accommodation—would further isolate and threaten to sap the vitality of this growing community. However, as Dr. Mark Hyman suggested, "The power of community to create health is far greater than any physician, clinic, or hospital."[30] Whether fully conscious of its power to heal or not, the African American enclave remained vital and resilient through self-reliance and a pioneering spirit.

Eight Mile Road runs along the surveyor's baseline that established the borders of Michigan's township system during the nineteenth century. In metropolitan Detroit, the baseline served to separate the original thirty-six-square-mile Royal Oak Township in Oakland County to the north from Greenfield Township in Wayne County to the south of the baseline. In a sense, the West Eight Mile community can only be fully understood as

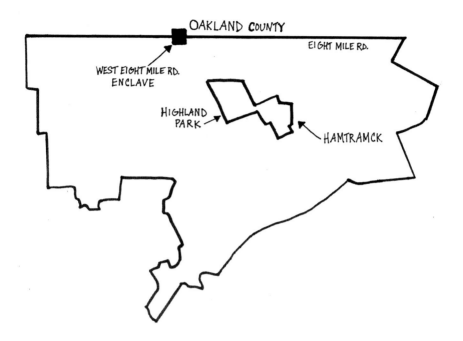

Ink drawing of Detroit boundaries, 1941. *Lauren Gohl.*

two halves of a larger one-square-mile whole, the present half-square-mile Royal Oak Township north of Eight Mile and the half-square-mile African American neighborhoods to the south. Although both communities have unique historical moments, they are aligned closely by race, by culture and by shared experiences.

THE ORIGINS OF MODERN ROYAL OAK TOWNSHIP

Royal Oak Township wasn't always a hamlet and wasn't always African American. Its history follows a complex path to the present day. Under the ordinance of 1785, the federal government proclaimed civil townships, each thirty-six square miles, as the basic unit of land management. The area directly north of today's West Eight Mile was described in an 1817 survey as "irreclaimable, and must remain forever unfit for culture or occupation, and must remain in the possession of wild beasts."[31] On December 5, 1819,

General Lewis Cass, the governor of the Michigan territory, set out to explore this forbidding territory on his way to sign a treaty with the Saginaw Indians. At a certain point, the governor was forced to leave behind his horse and slog through marshland with his party on foot. Upon approaching an old Ottawa Indian trail (Woodward Avenue), he established a road, which he marked as H, twelve miles north of Detroit, and paused to rest on solid ground under an oak tree. The governor was inspired to call the tree a Royal Oak, a conscious allusion to the legend of the original Royal Oak, located at Boscobel in Shropshire, England. In 1650, King Charles II hid in an old oak tree to elude the pursuit of Oliver Cromwell's men during the English Civil War. The tree became immortalized as the "Royal Oak" after Charles was able to regain the throne of England in 1660.

An act of the Legislative Council of the Territory of Michigan in 1832, which described the area as being located near an oak tree where Governor Cass and his party were to have rested, proclaimed it Royal Oak Township. The original oak tree, located at what is now the triangular intersection of Main, Rochester and Crooks Roads, was cut down in 1853. In June 1917, the Royal Oak Women's Club erected a marker that is now located at the entrance to Oakview Cemetery on Rochester Road.[32] The marker reads,

Royal Oak memorial marker, Royal Oak, Michigan. *Author's collection.*

"Near this spot stood the oak tree named by Governor Cass, the 'Royal Oak' from which Royal Oak Township received its name."

By this time, large numbers of migrants from the rural South had begun steadily arriving in the Detroit area in search of work and in response to deteriorating racial conditions in the former Confederate states. Most were directed to the segregated, working-class neighborhoods of Detroit's lower east side, but a few managed to bypass the overcrowded side streets of Black Bottom and settle north of the city in the unincorporated area around Eight Mile and Wyoming Roads. This was a remote area lacking city services, but because of housing restrictions within the city, there were few other choices where to live.

Both sides of rural Eight Mile Road became recognized as areas of black settlement. North of Eight Mile, the designated land was defined as Eight Mile, Detroyal, Forest Grove and Wyoming Park. Today, it is known as Eight Mile, Northend, Meyers Road and Mitcheldale. The area settled by African Americans was well known for its infestation of snakes, rabbits, skunks, hedgehogs, chipmunks, mud and slush, cranberry swamps and heavy forestation.

The thirty-six-square-mile township began to shrink beginning in 1921 with the incorporation of Berkley, Clawson, Royal Oak (the city), Hazel Park, Ferndale, Oak Park, Madison Heights, Pleasant Ridge and Huntington Woods. What remained of the original Royal Oak Township were two distinct, noncontiguous entities, one almost exclusively African American along Eight Mile Road and one to the north along Ten Mile Road. Much later, the northern tier of Royal Oak Township developed gradually into a largely middle-class area with a substantial Jewish settlement within its total population of 2,800 according to the 2000 U.S. Census. In 2004, this now largely ethnic Jewish community was annexed by Oak Park. During this entire period of incorporation, the African American area remained unwanted, unannexed and unincorporated.

World War II brought with it another surge of southern migration to Detroit. Nearly two thousand African Americans were moving into the Detroit area each month seeking war-related work, but few areas within highly segregated Detroit were capable of housing this tremendous influx. Agencies such as the FHA and Federal Public Housing Authority (FPHA) scrambled to find suitable locations for the construction of public and private housing specifically targeted for black war workers. The race riot of 1943 provided further impetus to the search, and soon the Eight Mile and Wyoming area in northwest Detroit came under considerable scrutiny.

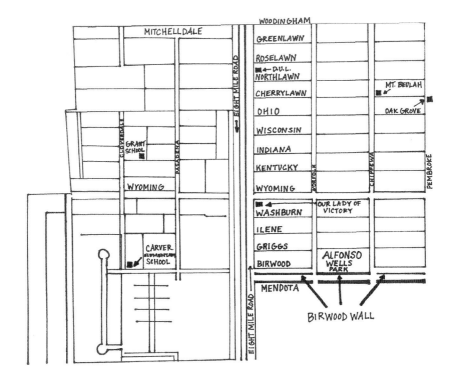

Ink drawing of West Eight Mile enclave. *Lauren Gohl.*

Both the Detroit Housing Commission and the City Planning Commission had already taken the position that the area could be used for temporary war housing as part of a larger postwar redevelopment plan. However, with the FHA now approving single-family home construction to the east of the Birwood Wall, only a few hundred temporary war housing units could be constructed.[33]

With fewer war housing units than anticipated slated for construction on the Detroit side of Eight Mile Road, attention focused on the area north along Wyoming Avenue in Royal Oak Township. The FPHA determined that sufficient vacant land was available for the construction of nearly 1,500 temporary war housing units, and construction soon began.[34] The large population of African Americans now living in purportedly "temporary" wartime housing in southern Oakland County would pose unanticipated issues in the years ahead for the neighboring communities of Ferndale and Oak Park and thrust them onto the national stage.

Chapter 2

HOUSING BARRIERS

Today, a casual walk down Mendota, the street on the other side of the Birwood Wall, brings into view a handful of abandoned, gutted structures among the otherwise well-kept brick bungalows that line both sides south to Pembroke Avenue. The formal abolition of restrictive covenant enforcement in 1948 gradually brought about the breakdown of the color line established by the Birwood Wall, and blacks have been buying properties on both sides of the wall since the early 1950s. Blockbusting and the threat of school busing frightened enough white home owners to sell during a wave of white flight. As Saul Alinsky cynically observed, "A racially integrated community is a chronological term timed from the entrance of the first black family to the exit of the last white family." After the 1967 racial rebellion, the timing accelerated dramatically.

When the Birwood Wall was constructed in 1941, Detroit's housing crisis had already reached the city's outskirts. In the immediate neighborhoods to the east and south of the West Eight Mile community, housing had reached near maximum density. To the west, the new whites-only subdivision was being platted. The frustrations and fears of hundreds of residents of the African American community were finding a voice in the outspoken leaders of both the Carver Progressive Club and Eight Mile Road Civic Association. The construction of the Birwood Wall had made clear that the FHA was not interested in making any significant breakthroughs with respect to racial integration. But perhaps the two neighborhood associations could broker a deal with the federal authorities whereby some relief, in the form of FHA-backed mortgage loans, could remedy the deteriorating housing conditions in the forty-two-square-block area that the HOLC's residential security maps had outlined in red.

THE STORY OF A SUBURBAN SLUM

This optimistic vision for the community by its associations' leaders met formidable opposition by a number of reform-minded organizations that had very different visions and agendas for the area. Chief among these was the Citizens' Housing and Planning Council of Detroit (CHPC), with its offices in the 1928 Art Deco masterpiece the Penobscot Building in downtown Detroit. In 1939, white sociologist Marvel Daines was dispatched to the area to report on social, economic and physical conditions.

Her report, entitled "Be It Ever So Tumbled: The Story of a Suburban Slum," describes the settlement as little more than "shacks of the most miserable character—unpainted, dilapidated, and in many cases practically in ruins." A brief history of the area that followed suggests that the black pioneers who settled the area, having migrated from the South with little money and less knowledge of construction requirements for a cold northern climate, built these flimsy domiciles with little outside assistance and, in the main, with sweat equity. Even before the author presents statistical data that is at the heart of the report, she cannot help but reveal her condescending attitude toward the residents of the area by recording all conversations in the exaggerated patois of uneducated southern blacks. One resident is quoted explaining why construction was so inadequate: "It done took four yeahs to get da house up, 'count we hadda pay fifteen hundr'd dollahs fo' de naked lan', an' we didn' have nothin' lef' fo' de lumbah."[35]

Despite the paternalistic tone that permeates the fifty-two-page pamphlet, the statistical data presented offer a window into the conditions in which residents were living. For example, of the 1,781 parcels of land that make up the Eight Mile–Wyoming area, 1,287, or 72 percent, were still vacant. More than 90 percent of existing structures were detached single-family units, of which 60 percent were built before 1924. Only 16 percent of these homes were in good condition, with three in ten requiring major repair. Fewer than half of the dwellings had a toilet and bath. Given the overall condition, seven in ten homes were rated "substandard" by the Real Property Inventory and Housing Survey, completed in 1938 by the Detroit Housing Commission.[36]

The interview portion of the report was intended to reveal the "human side" of the community, a side that naked statistics were not likely to reveal. The strategy was simple. Daines would interview the adult occupants of every tenth house in the forty-two-block area bounded by Eight Mile to the north, Woodingham Drive to the east, Pembroke to the south and Birwood to the west. Since there were 469 families living in the area, 48 would be contacted. With 10 percent of the residents interviewed, certain conclusions could be extrapolated.

The intent of the interviews, as expressed in the report's introduction, was to answer variations of the same question: "Why don't they keep their homes in better condition?" and "Why have they let them run down until they are an eyesore to the surrounding neighborhoods?" The logical fallacy of the questions, of course, is that they include the presumption of guilt and, ultimately, serve the author's (and agency's) agenda. To this end, Daines requested of each homeowner specific information regarding sources, types and amounts of income; number and kinds of automobiles owned; and personal characteristics such as hobbies and church affiliations:

It is amazing to see how far a factory wage can go—how many dozen pairs of shoes it can buy a year, how many growing young bodies it can clothe, how many hungry little mouths it can feed.

"I have to scrimp each month to make ends meet," Mrs. Appleton told me. "But these young ones are worth all the hours I spend making their clothes and figuring out how to buy the things they need."

Mr. Appleton works in a factory and earns $30 a week. They are an intelligent couple and are proud of their children. They have reason to be—. The children were at home eating their lunch when I visited. One goes to school and the other four range from one to six years of age. They are extremely attractive children—wide-eyed, well-mannered, spotlessly dressed. Their home is of the better type, with plastered walls nicely decorated, a furnace, bath, and modern kitchen. The furnishings are attractive and in excellent taste.

"We know we shouldn't be paying $30 a month rent on our income," Mrs. Appleton admitted to me, "but we did want a decent place for the children. We like it here—it's a nice neighborhood—but it keeps me busy figuring out how to give them all the other things I want them to have."[37]

Daines's conclusion was one of simple economics: the City of Detroit can no longer afford to subsidize the slum that the West Eight Mile community had become, especially given its history of delinquent or unpaid property taxes; the high cost of educating 386 black children at Higginbotham School; operating Birdhurst Recreation Center; maintaining streets, lighting and sewers; and providing fire and police protection. Daines disclaimed any preference for either of the two solutions offered, but she managed nonetheless to undercut the first one by suggesting the unlikelihood of it ever succeeding. The two solutions are: (1) The area may remain Negro but with rehabilitation mandatory, and (2) The area could be converted into a white neighborhood. The first solution proposes a low-cost housing project underwritten by the federal government or a privately funded housing project, or a plan whereby welfare houses would be constructed and maintained by the Department of Public Welfare. All three scenarios, Daines confessed, are found to be untenable.

The second solution, converting West Eight Mile to a white neighborhood, is presented as being the more reasonable alternative. The neighborhoods to the east and south, already white, range from lower-middle to upper-middle class, thus providing the city with a substantial upgrade to the area's tax base. Not to ignore the needs of the displaced black homeowners, Daines suggested the city find a "comparable area to the Eight Mile Road development," close to an industrial center of employment where blacks have already settled and garden space is available. A development of small cottages using salvaged materials and WPA labor would likely flourish in such circumstances. Before bringing the report to a close with a poem by Lewis Alexander entitled "The Prayer of the Dark Brother," Daines expressed confidence that, if made aware of all the facts, blacks would wholeheartedly endorse such a solution.[38]

Another major obstacle to making the West Eight Mile area eligible for FHA financing was a byproduct of the United States' entry into World War II. On the homefront, Detroit would rebound from the decade-long economic slump brought on by the Great Depression and return to its former status as an industrial boomtown by producing 10 percent of all war armaments with only 2 percent of the nation's population. "Just as Detroit was a symbol of America in peace," a 1942 story in *Forbes* declared, "so it is the symbol of America at war. Other towns make arms, as other towns make automobiles, but whether we win this war depends in great measure on Detroit."[39] Henry Ford would build the world's largest factory at Willow Run, just west of Detroit, to produce half of the military's B-24 bombers employed during the war. During its peak production, Willow Run would turn out a bomber every fifty-five minutes, twenty-four hours a day, seven days a week. Ford would need forty-two thousand dedicated

Oakdale Housing Project, located at Eight Mile and Wyoming, circa 1950. *Walter P. Reuther Library, Archives of Labor and Urban Affairs, Wayne State University.*

employees to keep the lines humming. Detroit's Cadillac plant converted from civilian car manufacture to tanks in fifty-five days. Other facilities produced tanks, radar units, field kitchens, amphibious vehicles and jeeps. Tens of thousands of war production workers were needed to fill the factory floors, and once again the American South would be recruited heavily to fill the bill. Two thousand African Americans per month were moving into the Detroit area, but the tightly segregated black neighborhoods could not possibly absorb the influx.

The housing crisis in Detroit did not go unnoticed in Washington, D.C. Both the Federal Public Housing Authority (FPHA) and the FHA were having difficulty finding housing sites to accommodate black war workers. Neither of the federal agencies nor local area municipalities were interested in integrated war housing projects that might otherwise have relieved some of the overcrowding. The black enclave of West Eight Mile eventually drew the attention of both federal agencies. Meanwhile, the Detroit Housing Commission (DHC) and the City Planning Commission (CPC) had concluded that the area was a prime candidate for comprehensive redevelopment planning. In the short term, the DHC believed the area was a perfect fit for locating up to 2,500 temporary war housing units. Add to this mix the for-profit Wayne County Better Homes, a construction company founded by African American business leaders and led by state senator Charles C. Diggs. The company had just successfully constructed 25 houses near the Sojourner Truth permanent defense housing project and was looking for additional sites to construct permanent housing for African Americans.[40]

A DIFFERENT KIND OF A WALL IN ROYAL OAK TOWNSHIP

Regarding barriers of segregation, things were not much different on the north side of Eight Mile Road. The Royal Oak community was ringed with institutional property, light industry, non-through streets and high fences. Through this deftly crafted suburban "wall," the Royal Oak Township community was isolated from its neighbors on all sides.

The Detroit Housing Commission, operating on an avowed segregationist policy, had the responsibility from the federal government for renting 1,464 dwelling units to African American war worker families. Detroit, being in a different county than the township, was alleged to have transferred some of its own chronic welfare cases and to have placed the poorest risks into the adjacent county of jurisdiction.[41] While war workers and their families doubled up in homes in the eastern half of the area utilizing garages, sheds and attics, it was not until January 1943 that the first family moved into the new war housing.

After many residents settled into the temporary war housing units, the federally appointed housing manager became aware of adjustment problems in the use of household facilities. The Detroit Urban League provided a tenant relations director to help residents who were having difficulties. A number of residents were unfamiliar with how to utilize their toilets and operate the stoves. Residents were afraid of using the gas stove and cooked outdoors on barbecue grills. This resident support service helped them to adjust to some of their physical needs. Little provision was made for educational and vocational development. Even basic sewage needs were ignored, for there was no sewer system. The housing manager's report to the federal government reported that fecal matter was traveling throughout the neighborhood. No attention was paid to the request for action to address the problem.[42]

The housing conditions in Royal Oak Township were unusual in many ways. For example, considering the dwelling units in the township, the United Community Services reported that 78.7 percent of all homes in the township were built in 1940 or later. Less than 1 percent (0.07) of all homes were built in 1919 or earlier. This was one of the newest communities in the metropolitan area when you consider that over 80 percent of its population and housing had been generated during the war years. Yet by 1950, according to the United States Census, three quarters or 1,709 of 2,300 housing units were either dilapidated or in need of major repair. At the same time, nearly half of the housing units were overcrowded—the worst overcrowding in the metropolitan area. In less than ten years, the population had grown sixfold, from 1,700 to 10,900.

Social workers recognized the strong division between the two black neighborhoods, one composed primarily of homeowners and the other temporary war housing tenants. There was little in the way of class distinctions, however, with only about twenty-five families considering themselves a "cut above" in post–World War II brick homes on Reimanville and Bethlawn at the Detroyal Park. The social workers racked their brains to find common projects around which residents from both areas could rally. Many residents from both communities felt closed off from the surrounding areas and often transacted business outside the township through intermediaries. Both neighborhoods faced similar needs and problems. They often expressed the belief that religion sustained them and prepared them for a better afterlife.

The Federal Housing Act of 1949 authorized the elimination of substandard housing in slum and blighted areas. It called for a redevelopment in order for every family to live in a "suitable living environment." Also, in 1949, the Supreme Court outlawed restrictive racial covenants. This heightened the fears of neighboring white communities. Resistance by whites to integrate with blacks occurred at all levels. Although some enclave resident women worked in the homes of more affluent whites, relations between the two communities remained distant.

In 1953, the township government purchased 874 of the 1,464 dwelling units from the Public Housing Administration (PHA) that had been constructed during the war as temporary housing. By June 1958, the township had made the final payment on the $181,000 mortgage. Now free and clear, the units—and most importantly the land on which they sat—served as equity for the one-third local contribution to urban renewal required by the

Gloria Butler, enjoying a summer day on North End Street, Royal Oak Township, 1951. Temporary war housing project can be seen in the background. *Gloria Butler.*

Federal Housing Act. The remaining 590 units were reclassified by the PHA as permanent units and sold to the Oakdale Residents Cooperative in June 1955 for $1,443,875 on a fifteen-year mortgage.[43]

The majority of housing built since 1945 was concentrated on the third blocks (north from Eight Mile Road) of Reimanville, Bethlawn and Mitchelldale. All of those units were considered sound, and most were sold under the Veterans Administration guarantee or insured by the Federal Housing Administration.

One of the major urban renewal project objectives was to increase homeownership in the area to at least 60 percent (from an estimated 20 to 30 percent in the late 1950s). This also implied a reduction in the number of renters, subsequently accomplished by the freezing of rental units of the now township-owned temporary war housing units, renamed Township Homes. In 1958, the population of the township had been reduced by about 500 residents. By the end of 1960, there remained fewer than 134 families in these units. The timeline was for the 874 units to be completely deprogrammed by July 1, 1961.The assistant manager of Township Homes reported that the majority of families moved to Detroit, with lesser numbers to Highland Park. A limited number expressed interest in finding a way to establish permanent residence within the community. Township Homes was thereafter razed to clear the site for public bidding. The planning objective was to sell the vacant land (in determined parcels) to developers for construction of new housing. The primary zoning of the area east of Wyoming was residential single family (R-1). The northern boundary of this area (North End) was zoned for light industry. The Eight Mile Road frontage maintained its zoning for business and commerce. The projected zoning of the 83.7 acres of land owned by the township west of Wyoming was single- and multi-dwelling.

The Federal Housing and Home Financing Act of 1954 mandated that citizen participation be part of the planning and approval process to qualify for urban renewal funding. To facilitate the program, urban renewal committees were established that would deal with the specific problems involved. Committees formed were Relocation, Rehabilitation, Building, Business, Senior Citizens and Finance. Early on, there was general agreement that any renewal of the local environment had to include paved streets, sidewalks, drainage, utilities, new housing, rehabilitation for others and landscaping.

The organization of block clubs was an especially crucial component of the process, for the general community had to be on board with all the coming changes. These were especially difficult to organize and maintain among the renters occupying the temporary housing units, however, not simply because of a lack of interest but because many of the renters were not there long enough to become committed to any community activity.

In March 1959, the General Development Plan was adopted by the township board. The physical plan as adopted called for a complete renewal of the area in about twenty years; creation of an industrial and commercial area; reduction of population to almost half; and development of play areas, a civic center and new single and multiple dwellings. The community's share of the urban renewal cost was to be derived from the sale of land owned by the local government, on which a good portion of the temporary war housing was situated.

The Urban Renewal Program (which had been officially amended for the seventh time by 1972) was terminated under "close-out procedures" as a federally supported urban renewal project as of 1975. Project activities remaining would thereafter fall under the township's community development department.[44]

FHA APPROVAL

Raymond Foley, the state director of the FHA, had already approved mortgage insurance for forty-five homes for black war workers in River Rouge, an industrial downriver suburb south of Detroit. Under the right circumstances, he was willing to approve FHA mortgage insurance for permanent private home construction in the Eight Mile–Wyoming area, but he also needed to address the issue of temporary public war housing. During the fall of 1943 and spring of 1944, Foley conducted meetings with the various organizations, including the two organizations that represented the interests of the area's current residents. Before making any kind of decision, Foley personally visited the enclave and concluded that its residents had worked hard to develop the area independent of federal or local assistance. Thus, in March 1944, a compromise was reached that seemed to satisfy most of the parties to the dispute: the DHC would locate 600 units of temporary public war housing within the southernmost section of the area, and private homes with FHA financing could be built to the north; also, 1,464 temporary public units for black war workers would be moved across Eight Mile Road into Royal Oak Township. It was a stunning, if not long overdue, victory for residents of the West Eight Mile area.[45]

Extending the FHA mortgage programs to African Americans in the West Eight Mile area represented a significant policy breakthrough. By 1950, more than 1,500 single family homes had been constructed in the area. In 1940, 70 percent of area dwellings were owner occupied; by 1960, it was 88 percent. Whether black owned or white owned, neighborhoods were solidifying. However, any suggestion that attitudes within neighboring white communities were evolving would be mistaken. Even Raymond Foley, the Michigan FHA director who engineered the local change in mortgage insurance eligibility, believed in the efficacy of racially homogenous communities, fearing the likelihood of confrontation and violence in mixed neighborhoods. In racially homogenous neighborhoods, which both races were thought to have preferred, property values stabilized; in mixed neighborhoods, they were likely to decline.

In 1941, the construction of the Birwood Wall represented symbolic affirmation of the social and economic necessity for formal barriers between homogenous racial groups. It mattered little that Marvel Daines's report to the CHPC had tallied thirty-seven white families, or 8 percent, living within the West Eight Mile community. The fact that these families were clustered on the west side of Woodingham Drive (the eastern boundary of the community) only reinforced the notion of an inborn predilection toward racial segregation.

Mr. Jones had a good job paying $30 a week with the City Asphalt Paving Department, and he too has a home which he is building—a large ten room house, which in its present state, he owns completely. However, the house is in the tar-paper stage, has no porch or steps or front door, a room for a bath but no fixtures, no inside doors, no plaster on the walls, and no hardware.

There is something rather admirable about this self-denying method of living—a creed which, perhaps because of necessity, demands that nothing be bought except for cash. Mr. and Mrs. Jones have ten children ranging from ten months to 19 years. They got enough money together to put up the structure of their house—but had nothing left for plumbing, decorating, or furnishing. At the time I visited, they had been building the house for ten years, and probably would not be finished for another ten. They have no furniture except five beds, a few straight back-chairs, and a table. The living room is completely bare of furnishings.

As I talked to Mrs. Jones, the smaller children were eating lunch, which consisted of enormous plates of bean, and glasses of milk.

"Sometimes I wonder if we'll ever get the place done," she said a little wearily. "It takes so much for food."

Here was another case where the house was being built by "two bits worth here and two bits worth there"—a long drawn-out process of doing without actual necessities and eating beans entirely too often—in order to have a few cents left each week for a door handle or a fixture or a piece of lumber![46]

JEWISH NEIGHBORS, ONCE AGAIN

Beginning in the 1930s, Jews began migrating to northwest Detroit, in small numbers, from Dexter-Davison, at that time the center of Jewish activity. As the migration progressed, the epicenter of settlement became the neighborhoods surrounding Bagley Elementary School, located halfway between Six to the south and Seven Mile Roads to the south and north, Livernois to the east and Wyoming to the east and west.

Decades earlier, large numbers of ethnic Jews had moved from their original Hastings Street neighborhood, where the majority of Jews resided at the time, to neighborhoods to the north and west of Woodward, converging on Twelfth Street for a time and then onto Warren and Oakland before settling into Dexter-Davison on the near west side. Detroit's blacks would often move into areas vacated by Jews in what Sidney Fine termed "a pattern of racial succession rather than integration."[47] Jews had come to realize that mobility was made easy, in part, because blacks represented a "ready made" housing market. Facing potential resistance and often violence in the housing market west of Woodward, blacks experienced little such resistance from Jews wanting to move on. Later, when Jews began moving north from Dexter-Davison to northwest Detroit, the same process unfolded.

Through the 1940s and 1950s, Jews and blacks lived harmoniously in adjacent space. Real estate developer Harry Slatkin had tried unsuccessfully to create a substantial barrier, like the Birwood Wall, along Pembroke Avenue in 1953. When the city building department denied his request for a permit to, in essence, close off the black enclave from his newly built homes and apartment buildings to the south, Slatkin had to satisfy himself that the eight-foot-high wooden stockade fence he erected would serve the same purpose.

When black families began moving into neighborhoods south of Pembroke and west of Birwood in the 1950s, activity was closely monitored by neighborhood associations. Joseph Fauman, who had joined the staff of the Jewish Community Council (JCC) in the late 1940s as a community relations specialist, had become a member of the Blenheim Forest District Improvement Association (BFDIA). He had learned to use his expertise to defuse tensions associated with school and residential integration. Now as recording secretary for the BFDIA, he was feeling compromised. As a staff member deeply committed to the ideals of the JCC, whose credo included developing sound neighborhoods that were open to all without regard to race, creed, color or national origin, Fauman was working closely with members of the neighborhood association who were expressing increased concern over the irreparable damage that was being done by the "infiltration" of black families in their neighborhoods. The association board even proposed going so far as purchasing homes as they came onto the market and reselling them to more "desirable" clientele. In one specific incident, one hundred local residents gathered for the sole purpose of pooling resources to purchase a home that, rumor had it, was going to be bought by a black family. Only the fact that the group was unable to raise the necessary funds allowed the black family to complete the purchase.[48]

An abiding concern of many Jewish residents in northwest Detroit was that as much as they generally did not want to appear racist or engage in some of the vitriolic discourse, they most certainly did not want to fall victim to the blame game. Many remembered quite vividly the pattern of neighborhood succession, as well as the discrimination they experienced themselves while moving into certain neighborhoods. In 1959, the Ruritan Park South Civic Association, representing communities even farther south, secured strong support among local residents for a written "option agreement." Once signed, residents were honor bound to seek the association's approval before selling their home to a prospective buyer. The document was intended as an informal "restrictive covenant" that carried no legal weight, for such had been ruled unconstitutional and therefore unenforceable in 1948. But it just might generate enough red tape at the time of purchase to discourage unwanted buyers.[49]

Also in 1959, M-10, the Lodge Freeway, was completed. The newest Detroit freeway cut a ribbon through northwest Detroit, delivering commuters downtown to work and pleasure. In the opposite direction, the Lodge took commuters through Southfield, which bordered Oak Park and Huntington Woods, two Oakland County suburbs experiencing an influx of Jewish families. After the 1967 Detroit racial rebellion, the migration of Jews into suburbs north of Eight Mile Road was largely indiscriminate, with significant clusters settling in Southfield, West Bloomfield, Bloomfield Hills, Royal Oak and Farmington Hills, as well as the earlier settlements of Oak Park and Huntington Woods. By 1976, there were nearly eighty thousand Jews in metropolitan Detroit, with most having departed the city of Detroit.[50]

THE SOJOURNER TRUTH HOUSING RIOT

At the time the Birwood Wall was completed in August 1941, no incidents of racial violence directly attributable to its construction were reported. The real estate developer had, in fact, been confronted by members of the Carver Progressive Club, but nothing further came of it. Racial turmoil had erupted the previous year in other parts of the city involving school integration and Belle Isle recreation. In February 1940, a racial altercation occurred between black and white students at Northwestern High School at Lawton and Tireman, north of the expanding black west side. The incident arose over a false narrative that black enrollment in the spring semester was threatening to turn away white students; in fact, the numbers had remained stable for years: 3,300 white, 700 black. The concern among white students curiously reflected the views of local realtors who were trying to restrict further black incursion north of Tireman. Order was quickly restored when Mayor Edward Jeffries, police and school officials, in concert with the Northwest Pastors Association and the NAACP, intervened by working with parents to address the situation at home.[51]

Five months later, over the Fourth of July holiday, a black youth allegedly took a canoe belonging to someone else. After he returned it under order of a nearby patrolman, the youth ran, was apprehended and was beaten in front of hundreds of black picnickers. The incident further escalated at the police station, where angry protesters who had witnessed the beating scuffled with police. Two protesters were arrested. The black youth, Melvin McConico, was sentenced by a Recorder's Court judge to thirty days in the House of Correction; the two protesters were fined and placed on probation.[52]

These two isolated incidents did not reflect the much deeper issue that inadequate housing was creating for African Americans in various parts of the city. As the federal government constructed housing projects, such as the Brewster-Douglass Projects on the east side, black and white defense workers competed elsewhere for limited accommodations in a city with a 99 percent occupancy rate. In May 1941, the Division of Defense Housing Coordination (DDHC) recommended the construction of one thousand government-financed family units, with two hundred of these units, on the recommendation of the Detroit Housing Commission, set aside for black occupancy. After much wrangling between local and federal authorities, a site for black war production workers was agreed on: a sparsely settled, mixed neighborhood of twenty acres on the city's northeast side. Close to the proposed development, just five city blocks west, was Conant Gardens, a subdivision of middle-class black homeowners. The community was served by Pershing High School and Atkinson School, both predominantly black. Polish immigrants had settled the area as well in order to work in such factories as Dodge main. Just south was the city of Hamtramck, with a heavy concentration of Polish Americans.

The controversy began when members of the Conant Garden Homeowners' Association (CGHA) approached white homeowners who resided immediately south of the proposed housing project, just east of Ryan Road. Believing that the housing project involved the construction of unsightly temporary barracks, eventually attracting unsavory businesses and clientele, the CGHA felt compelled to act on an issue deemed to be one of class, not race. The alliance formed at a June 24 meeting between hundreds of CGHA members and neighboring white homeowners was short-lived. Upon learning that the housing project was to involve the construction of permanent, not temporary units, and realizing that much of the angst expressed by the white homeowners was racially tinged, the CGHA backed off its opposition to the project.

Sojourner Truth Public Housing Project, Detroit, 1942. *Library of Congress.*

Sign across the street from the Sojourner Truth Housing Project. *Library of Congress.*

From the perspective of the working-class Polish Catholics, who were concentrated around St. Louis the King Parish Church, the temporary alliance had galvanized the local white community. Almost overnight, a Seven Mile–Fenelon Homeowners Association was born with one principal objective: to pressure federal and local officials to reverse their decision to locate the project at Nevada and Fenelon and to select an alternative site.

In September, the Detroit Housing Commission sent signals to both communities, black and white, that the original plans were moving forward by formally naming the project after the ex-slave and abolitionist Sojourner Truth. However, with federal officials suggesting to white residents of the area that the issue of occupancy was not yet settled, neither side felt particularly reassured. Through December, the Seven Mile–Fenelon Homeowners Association engaged in picketing the future housing site, organizing a letter-writing campaign and issuing stern warnings of potential violence. By the middle of January, the strategies had borne fruit. Federal officials decided to assign the housing to whites while promising to find another site for a black housing project.

Whites picketing in an attempt to prevent African Americans from moving into Sojourner Truth Housing Project. *Library of Congress.*

The reaction within the black community was as swift as it was predictable. The NAACP, various church groups, the UAW and liberal white organizations rallied on behalf of restoring the original plan for black occupancy of the housing project. The Catholic Church, however, assumed a neutral position, except for Polish clergy in the area. This local issue had gained national attention, and a local delegation traveled to Washington, D.C., to seek a meeting with President Roosevelt and pressure any administration official who would listen. The effort paid off, and occupancy was reassigned to blacks once again.

Left: African American males prepared to defend themselves during Sojourner Truth riot, 1942. *Library of Congress.*

Below: Sojourner Truth riot caused by whites attempting to prevent blacks from moving into new U.S. federal housing project. *Library of Congress.*

African Americans moving into the Sojourner Truth Housing Project, 1942. *Library of Congress.*

First family having moved into the Sojourner Truth Housing Project, 1942. *Library of Congress.*

February 28 was set as the move-in date for the first 24 black families. Both sides were poised for confrontation, and nobody was surprised when more than 1,000 individuals, both white and black, engaged in violent skirmishes. At least 40 individuals were injured, and 200 arrests were made before an exclusively white police force was able—or willing—to restore order. Only 3 of the 109 rioters held over for trial were white. The degree of racism among Detroit's finest was put on public display as photographs and firsthand accounts began to filter out, exposing a level of police brutality that shocked many.

THE 1943 RACE RIOT

Although the violent confrontation at Nevada and Fenelon sent shock waves throughout the municipal offices downtown, it had been contained to a single neighborhood and, fortunately, no one had been killed. This was not the case a year later, on June 20, when a racial conflict on Belle Isle, the nation's largest city-owned island park, escalated quickly and spread downtown. After federal troops were called in to restore order, the tally of death, injury and property destruction was staggering: 43 killed, 433 injured and millions of dollars in property damage, particularly in areas of high black residential concentration. More than 1,800 individuals were arrested for looting and other infractions. Social psychologist Roger Brown, who was a high school student in Detroit at the time, recalls the buildup of tension preliminary to the outburst: African American resentment had deepened not only because of the worsening wartime housing crisis and employment discrimination but also because of particular segregation practices that arose during the war. The Red Cross, for example, barred black donors as early as December 1941 and relented later, only reluctantly, by accepting—but segregating—African American blood donations. In the navy, blacks were typically given the most menial jobs on board; the Marine Corps would not even accept African Americans. The indignities went on. There were strains for Detroit's white population as well, especially, as Brown recalled, "for the Southern whites who had come to Detroit for war-related work and were not accustomed to the degree of equality that prevailed there, to unsegregated public transportation and partially unsegregated recreational facilities."[53]

The specific event that triggered the riot was lost in the fog of the evening's chaos, but witnesses suggest that a fight broke out between small groups of whites and blacks. The free-for-all spread to the MacArthur Bridge (or, more popularly, the Belle Isle Bridge), which connected the island to the city, and the violence spread into downtown. Fueling the conflict were unsubstantiated rumors circulating on both sides of Woodward Avenue. Two individuals told a crowd of black patrons at the Forest Social Club, at 700 Forest Avenue, that a mob of whites had thrown a black baby and its mother off the bridge. On the west side of Woodward, the white side, the riot was inflamed by a rumor that blacks had raped and murdered a white woman on the bridge. Roving black and white gangs perpetrated random acts of violence, such as pulling people from automobiles and streetcars; shooting or beating bystanders; looting shops, particularly along Hastings Street; and generally engaging in guerrilla warfare. Mercifully, there was little arson due to wartime gasoline rationing.

The riot was quelled after President Roosevelt sent six thousand federal troops to patrol Detroit's streets at the urgent request of Governor Harry Kelly and Mayor Jeffries. In the aftermath, Jeffries praised the police for

Cars burn near Stimpson Street during the 1943 race riot, June 21. *Walter P. Reuther Library, Archives of Labor and Urban Affairs, Wayne State University.*

exercising restraint, even though seventeen blacks (and no whites) were killed at the hands of white patrolmen. The NAACP's Thurgood Marshall later called the police commissioner's enforcement policies weak and uneven, as 85 percent of those arrested were black and white atrocities were largely ignored. Any sober assessment of the violence and destruction that had occurred left one with questions: What did Detroit learn and what was it prepared to do about it?

THE 1967 RACIAL REBELLION

On January 2, 1962, Jerome "Jerry" P. Cavanagh was sworn in as mayor. Cavanagh, a Roman Catholic with undergraduate and law degrees from the Jesuit University of Detroit, defeated the incumbent Louis C. Miriani, who had lost support among many white voters disappointed with the city's fiscal performance despite high property taxes and disenchanted with his efforts to address issues within the black community. Cavanagh appealed to both voting blocs and made clear in his inaugural address that he would, first and foremost, address the city's fiscal crisis and, secondly, exert a "moral influence…not only as it relates to the problem of the negro, but to all citizens of Detroit."[54]

Cavanagh's overnight success in the arenas of both fiscal stability and race relations made him a media darling on both the local and national level. In March 1967, the national Municipal League described Detroit as an "All-American City" because under Cavanagh's leadership the city's urban renewal and redevelopment—as illustrated by its gleaming $250 million cultural center—reversed decades of decline. Cavanagh, as well as New York City major John Lindsay, were seen as having national political futures.

While Cavanagh had revitalized Detroit on many fronts, he failed to address the concerns of the black underclass. Committees had been established to address unemployment, job discrimination, housing, public education and even police-community relations, which had been a particular sore spot among African Americans in Detroit. But Cavanagh's administration, and these issue-oriented committees in particular, never really drilled down to establish lines of communication with individuals who had never been consulted: the city's black underclass forced to live in the only areas immediately available nearby, in substandard, overcrowded housing west of Woodward in Detroit's lower west side. The planning of slum clearance projects for freeway construction and upscale

A view of Twelfth Street on first day of civil rebellion, June 23, 1967. *Walter P. Reuther Library, Archives of Labor and Urban Affairs, Wayne State University.*

housing developments on the city's near east side did not properly address the thorny issue of relocation for the thousands of displaced families and individuals who lay in the path of bulldozers. More than eleven thousand homes, occupied mainly by low-income black citizens, were razed and replaced by housing units that better served middle- to high-income individuals. Relocation efforts were uncoordinated and inadequate, creating a new and volatile environment for an even further alienated underclass.

In the early morning hours of Sunday, July 23, 1967, a handful of Detroit police officers executed what they perceived to be a routine raid on a blind pig, Detroit jargon for an after-hours drinking establishment, at Twelfth and Clairmount. The second-story club was filled that night with individuals celebrating the return of two GIs who had just completed a tour of duty in Vietnam. An unexpectedly large party of eighty-two celebrants was taken into custody and paraded awkwardly onto Twelfth Street because the steel door in the back was padlocked. A small gathering outside on the hot, muggy morning, curious about the goings-on, soon grew to two hundred. As the size of the crowd changed, so did the mood. Unable to load all the partiers quickly into available paddy wagons, the police were confronted with threats, rock throwing and a pent-up desire to execute a bit of revenge on the symbols of municipal authority and repression. Pushing, kicking and screams of "police brutality" rang out, helping to create an atmosphere of disorder. The departure of the last paddy wagon at about 4:30 a.m. left a void of any social control. Localized unruliness quickly evolved into an ever-expanding gyre of rioting and property destruction that would last the better part of a week. The riot was largely a rebellion of blacks perennially victimized by an overly aggressive white police department that had inherited the mantle of brutality from previous generations of street patrolmen.

On many levels, Detroit never completely recovered from the 1967 rebellion. The dead were buried (43 of them, predominantly black), the wounds of the injured (nearly 1,200) eventually healed and much of the rubble was cleared, but businesses did not return. The police perpetrators were largely exonerated. And the city's reputation—locally, nationally and even internationally—was in tatters in less than a single week.

Chapter 3

BARRIERS TO EMPLOYMENT

The combined pull of good job prospects in the industrial North and the push from deplorable social conditions in the Jim Crow South became the tipping point for tens of thousands of blacks who made Detroit a primary destination between 1910 and 1950. The farm-to-city movement did not exclude intermediate stops in southern cities like Birmingham, Memphis and Atlanta, all of which experienced significant population growth between 1910 and 1930. But for large numbers of black families like the Crewses, who made such stopovers along their journey to Eight Mile Road, and for Antonio Rosa and Mary Gillem, who came from Ohio, the magnet of "real" opportunity lay farther north.

Detroit's population growth and physical expansion through annexation can only be characterized as staggering. Immigrants from abroad, who had fueled Detroit's insatiable desire for factory workers until the First World War, were replaced by migrants from the American South. In 1900, 285,704 people lived in Detroit; in 1910, 465,766; in 1920, 993,678; and in 1930, 1,568,662.[55] Detroit had become the fastest-growing metropolitan area in the country and was already the fourth-largest city in the United States by 1925. In an attempt to accommodate its ever-expanding population, Detroit engaged in a campaign of land annexation, but even that—as we have seen—could not keep pace with demands for decent, affordable housing. Annexation of land would transform the physical contours of the city. In 1905, the city encompassed 29 square miles; in 1915, 47; in 1922, 85; and by 1926, the last year of its program of annexation, the city of Detroit covered 119 square miles.[56]

The growth in the city's size and population, of course, was a reflection of its industrial expansion. By the mid-1920s, Greater Detroit had 3,000 major manufacturing plants, 37 automobile plants and at least 250 automobile suppliers. Although the automobile industry accounted for more than half of the city's total manufactured products, Detroit also produced adding machines, kitchen stoves, cigars, insulated wire, sheet copper and grass and many other products of industry.

The First World War had brought about employment opportunities to blacks heretofore almost completely unobtainable. Previously in Detroit, African Americans were engaged almost entirely in personal service occupations—janitor, porter, elevator operator, domestic, hotel waiter and so forth. From a purely business point of view, factory owners or superintendents were thought to be protecting their investments. The idea of using blacks in any appreciable number was considered ludicrous—the operating theory regarding blacks in the labor forces was that they were irremediably slothful and inefficient and that they could not stand the intensive demands of northern industry. Above all, it was believed that black and white did not mix on the factory floor, whether the white laborer was native or foreign-born.[57] Now, with the labor vacuum created by the wartime curb on immigration and therefore immigrant labor, need created opportunity.

Blacks migrating to Detroit for work found employment opportunities both during and after the war, although they suffered extreme levels of discrimination with respect to the nature of the work and opportunities for advancement. Factory foremen, regardless of the specific industry in Detroit, offered the black job applicant the hottest, dirtiest, noisiest, most physically exhausting and most dangerous job on the floor. Starting on the bottom more often than not led to staying on the bottom. Discrimination in wages earned or hours worked did not really apply. Wages and hours were more a function of the kind of work needed to be done. The worst jobs were paid the worst hourly wage. No white worker wanted these jobs and would have been forced into them only when necessary and, it was expected, only temporarily.

The automobile industry absorbed large numbers of black job applicants, though not equally among car companies or even within different plants of the same company. The first factories to integrate were Ford, Briggs and Dodge. Overall, two-thirds of blacks hired were classified as unskilled laborers, while the same was true for only one-fourth of whites. Such unskilled jobs included sweeping, tending the furnace and iron smelting and pouring; semi-skilled

Above and opposite: Factory workers, Briggs Manufacturing, Detroit. *Library of Congress.*

positions, when they were available, were limited to the most dangerous or undesirable, such as sand blaster, shear operator or heater.

Ford Motor Company, the largest single employer of African Americans, attempted to hire blacks in proportion to their presence in metropolitan Detroit's labor force. In 1926, this number was ten thousand. Ford attempted to disperse these black employees across all departments and occasionally even offered supervisory positions. Vertical movement within the company, on a

happenstance basis, was atypical. A conscious policy among industry leaders, including Ford Motor Company executives, guided hiring and placement decisions: blacks could work harmoniously with whites so long as they knew their place.

In 1916, Forrester B. Washington and Henry G. Stevens opened the first Detroit Urban League (DUL) office, an affiliate of the National Urban

League, which had been created earlier to solve some of the many problems black immigrants from the South were experiencing in the urban industrial centers. Its mission gradually expanded to include seeking employment and housing opportunities for blacks while offering a variety of social services, including healthcare and recreation.

The Detroit Urban League was funded, in part, by the Employers' Association of Detroit, which was formed at the turn of the century to defend factories against intrusions by organized labor. By 1910, unions were effectively dead, and the association was committed to preventing any resurrection. Funding the DUL came with a price tag. The DUL would operate an employment office, funneling migrant blacks to various Detroit factories on an as-needed basis. These newly employed blacks, knowing nothing about trade unionism, were malleable in the hands of management and could and would be used as strike breakers in time of labor agitation. The DUL never saw itself as an agency addressing issues of discrimination, like the NAACP. Instead, the DUL saw its mission in a very different light, as a coordinating agency assisting blacks adjust to life in the urban environment by providing assistance with employment, housing, healthcare and recreation.[58]

The path of employment for blacks in Detroit lay first in the automobile factories and foundries. Gradually, officials of the major Detroit utilities—Detroit Edison, Michigan Consolidated Gas and Michigan Bell Telephone—relaxed their hiring standards and began to accept qualified blacks. After this, banks and department stores followed suit. National Bank of Detroit and Detroit Bank and Trust were among the first Detroit-area banks to hire African Americans. J.L. Hudson Company, Detroit's premier department store, placed black women on its elevators, and the DUL saw this as a major opportunity for African Americans to serve as public ambassadors. Crowley's Department store next door soon began to place black women on its elevators as well. Gradually, a few black women were offered opportunities to work as salespersons. Their success led to further opportunities.[59]

HENRY FORD'S RECRUITMENT OF AFRICAN AMERICANS

Henry Ford's decision to pay his workers five dollars a day, at the urging of his business manager James Couzens, was born of fiscal necessity. In 1913, the year before the change, Ford had to hire fifty-two thousand workers just to keep his lines running with the required fourteen thousand. When Couzens explained the math—that a loyal, highly paid workforce would yield reductions in total labor costs by reducing worker turnover and production downtime—Ford was sold.[60]

But there was a catch. Ford's new offer of $5.00 for an eight-hour workday was contingent. Workers could accept the basic wage of $2.34 a day, but to earn the remaining $2.66 as a profit-sharing bonus, workers were required to meet two conditions: first, they had to be residents of the city of Detroit for at least six months; and second, they must submit to an investigation and possibly counseling from the company's newly created Ford Sociological Department. Ford wished to exert some measure of social control over his employees, insisting on desirable personal behaviors and satisfactory home conditions. About 75 percent of Ford workers were European and Russian immigrants, and in Ford's paternalistic point of view, they needed to be "Americanized" by learning English and developing an appropriate lifestyle.[61]

Following the United States' entry into the Second World War, foreign immigration—and the industrial workers it produced—slowed to a trickle due to restrictive immigration laws, just as it did during the First World War. Since Ford was beginning to hire large numbers of black migrants, Ford turned once again to the Sociological Department to screen and supervise its black workers. The issue became that the living conditions of black migrants and foreign immigrants differed dramatically from other workers. One example illustrates the problem for the Sociological Department. Many black men left families behind in the South to put down roots in the North. The plan was to eventually send for the wife and children. In the meantime, many black workers had taken common-law wives in Detroit, normally a circumstance in which the Department would intervene and insist on marriage for the cohabitating couple. In this instance, Ford Motor Company would be endorsing bigamy.

Henry Ford began to cultivate relationships with Detroit's most prominent black ministers for the ostensible purpose of screening black workers. However, tying those select ministers to Ford Motor Company served a broader purpose as well. To continue the pipeline of church-endorsed black applicants, the ministers were expected to support Ford's virulent anti-union stance. Ford tapped Robert Bradby of Second Baptist Church, who was perhaps the most influential black pastor in the city of Detroit; Father Everand Daniel of St. Matthew; and Reverend William Beck of Bethel AME Church. Many blacks, it has been speculated, joined one of these churches in the hopes of obtaining employment at Ford Motor Company.

Black employees at Ford Motor Company, as well as other industries throughout the city, were particularly receptive to anti-union propaganda, for organized labor had done little in the past to affirm their rights. Given the overt racism of many union members, such as those belonging to the American Federation of Labor, and the generally weak position of unionism in Detroit, blacks turned to a variety of other kinds of organizations, some more conservative, others more progressive, to help give voice to their employment issues. Such organizations as the NAACP and the Detroit Urban League recorded upticks in membership during the early to late 1920s, and newer, more progressive organizations such as the Good Citizen League and Marcus Garvey's Universal Negro Improvement Association were developing large followings. The UNIA, in particular, counted as many as five thousand members by 1922, and some of its marches demanding equal treatment drew crowds estimated at fifteen thousand. In addition, black Democratic clubs were starting to form as an alternative to existing Republican organizations.

In 1932, Mayor Frank Murphy, a Democrat who had even-handedly presided over the Ossian Sweet murder trial, which ended in an acquittal, endorsed Franklin Roosevelt for president, further linking his supportive black base to the Democratic Party. By the mid-1930s, Henry Ford's grip over the black working-class community had loosened considerably, and overtures from the more progressive factions of various unions were beginning to slice into the traditional black resistance to labor representation.

EIGHT MILE DURING THE GREAT DEPRESSION

Black migration into Detroit from outside the state had come to a virtual standstill during the Great Depression before it picked up again during the Second World War. The 120,066 blacks in Detroit in 1930 were facing especially hard times as more than 30 percent of those on relief roles were black, owing in part to the private sector's mantra of "last hired, first fired," as well as other subtle discriminatory practices. At the same time, FDR's Works Progress Administration (WPA), formed on May 6, 1935, provided gainful employment to millions of largely unskilled workers to carry out such broad infrastructure projects as the construction of municipal buildings, roads, bridges and pipelines.

The black enclave along Eight Mile Road was not exempt from the disproportionate effects of the Depression on black Americans. In 1941, in the hours before Detroit was to become a wartime boomtown and Birwood Street would see a wall constructed in its backyard, half of the enclave's families were relief recipients in one form or the other: 20 received old age benefits, 60 welfare assistance, 20 aid to dependent children and 140 were participating in WPA public works projects. Welfare beneficiaries also received sacks of flour, beans, sugar and other staples. Those who were regularly employed drew their paychecks from miscellaneous work or from positions with the City of Detroit. Miscellaneous work included 70 who worked for the Ford Motor Company, 10 with the Briggs factory, 10 with the Ford service department, 40 in construction work and 40 working in local stores or providing personal services such as beauty parlor or barbershop employment. Another 20 individuals neither worked nor received any form of relief.[62]

By this time, half of all African Americans working in the metropolitan area were employed by the Ford Motor Company in one capacity or another. Nearly one-third of the employed black males in the Eight Mile enclave were working at one or other Ford facilities. Generally speaking, however, blacks refused to sign union cards—not because they any longer felt indebted to Henry Ford for giving them jobs but because the old American Federation of Labor's (AFL's) auto workers union failed to treat blacks as equals.

The turning point for unions came in 1935 with the formation of the Congress of Industrial Organizations (CIO), now a rival to the AFL. The CIO's United Auto Workers had a strict policy of racial equality, and blacks started to listen. A series of sit-down strikes began in 1936, the most famous and effective of which occurred at the GM plant in Flint that lasted nearly two months. By that time, Governor Frank Murphy—long remembered by blacks as the fair-minded judge who presided over the Ossian Sweet murder trial and, subsequently, as the mayor of Detroit—acted as mediator and negotiated recognition of the UAW by General Motors. After a similar sit-down strike the next month at a Chrysler facility, that automaker formally recognized the UAW as well.

However, the jewel in the crown would be recognition by Ford Motor Company, but it would not come as swiftly as it had at GM and Chrysler. On May 26, 1937, several workers attempting to organize a union at the Ford Rouge plant, the largest manufacturing facility in the world, were severely beaten by agents of the Ford Service Department, managed by Harry Bennett, in what has become known in labor lore as the "Battle of

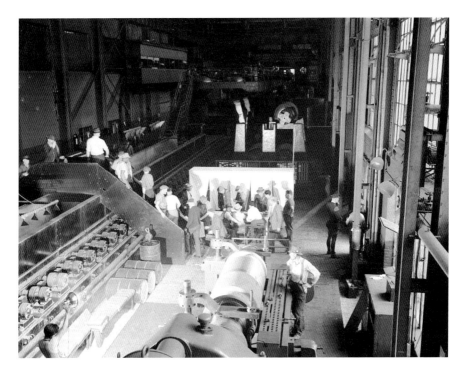

Election of officers to Ford Local 600, United Automobile Workers, Congress of Industrial Organizations. Eighty thousand River Rouge Plant workers voted. *Library of Congress.*

the Overpass." It would take until 1941 when black employees, who made up 20 percent of Dearborn's massive Rouge complex, would resolve their long-standing ambivalence toward unions. Blacks signed union cards and agreed to be represented by UAW Local 600. On April 1, 1941, a walkout by Ford workers protesting Harry Bennett's firing of eight union members shut down the Rouge plant. After several days of impasse, Henry Ford—partly at the goading of his wife, Clara—finally agreed to recognize the UAW and signed a collective bargaining agreement with Local 600.[63]

Union representation was a distinct step forward for many blacks, although a disproportionate number continued to work in the most dangerous, soul-crushing areas (River Rouge's foundry was often referred to as "the black department"). With wartime Detroit shifting production to war materiel, blacks could only hope that their sacrifices in the war effort—both in the military and on the homefront—would pave the way to a more egalitarian future. In 1942, a twenty-six-year-old, James G. Thompson of Wichita, Kansas, penned an impassioned letter to the *Pittsburgh Courier*, the most

Ford auto workers, Local 600, vote on officers. *Library of Congress*.

widely circulated African American newspaper in the United States. He suggested that blacks who were willing to sacrifice their lives in the struggle with foreign enemies were still being treated as second-class citizens at home. He therefore proposed that while the rest of America adopt the "V for Victory" sign, African Americans should adopt the "double V" to promote victory over both enemies from within and outside America.[64]

The years after the war saw an opportunity in Detroit for working-class blacks to ascend to the middle class. With the 1951 "Treaty of Detroit," which the UAW negotiated with General Motors, workers black and white won comprehensive health insurance, pensions, cost-of-living adjustments and income protection during economic downturns. Ford and Chrysler, flush as well with huge profits in the postwar economy, followed suit. None foresaw the serious threat from Japan on the horizon. But there were other, more immediate threats to Detroit's employment picture—particularly black employment—that only a few prescient individuals within leadership roles at UAW Local 600 could foresee.

EMPLOYMENT OPPORTUNITIES IN ROYAL OAK AFTER THE WAR

In Royal Oak Township, the rapid population increase during World War II created new social problems. After the war, high unemployment and economic unrest set the stage for community decline.

Employment opportunities with the township were extremely limited. There was not a single industry within the township after the war. The two schools and the forty-five business establishments represented the largest employers within the community. However, 96 percent of the school employees and an estimated 85 percent of business employees lived outside the township. It was also estimated that 75 percent of the owners of businesses were non-residents of the township. The largest single employer in the township was the township government, which employed a very small percentage of the total population. In other words, the vast majority of residents had to seek employment outside the immediate community. Most of the men and women commuted to Detroit or to a suburban city for employment.

The 1956 Township Survey reported that out of a township civilian labor force of 2,279 males and 660 females, 76 percent of the males were employed in the service and labor categories and 42 percent of the females were household workers. The survey figures showed also that less than one half of 1 percent of the total labor force was employed in the professional, proprietor and managerial categories.[65]

The State Employment Security office reported at the time a strong downward trend in the employment categories of unskilled and semi-skilled workers. With more than three-quarters of the male civilian labor force of the township in the unskilled and semi-skilled categories, the employment possibilities for residents looked bleak. Aside from these local trends in employment categories reported by the Employment Security office, the citizens of the township were also faced with the factor of race and educational limitations.

Within the township, there were no public or private facilities for industrial training. Neither were there any planned apprenticeship or on-the-job training programs sponsored by a public or private institution.

WRITING ON THE WALL

Back in Detroit, even as management and labor were celebrating the prospects of long-term labor stability in labor relations, officers with Local 600 saw the Ford Motor Company begin a strategy of laying off Rouge employees, ostensibly due to cancelled government orders, but actually replacing them with workers in unrepresented locations. So-called runaway plants were being established in the Midwest and the South. Local 600 members were called to a "protest meeting" on March 31, 1951, where it was revealed that nearly three-quarters of Rouge's 1,400 motor machinist jobs had been moved to Ohio plants. About 1,000 jobs were being lost each month at River Rouge. Local 600 viewed the steady loss of positions at the Rouge plant as a direct threat to the economic stability of Greater Detroit. Tensions began to rise not only between Local 600 and the Ford Motor Company but also between Local 600 and the National Ford Department of the UAW-CIO. The national office was much more concerned about overall employment numbers than those of individual sites such as the Rouge. Even the movement of machinery out of the Rouge plant was insufficient to generate much interest or support from the International Union.

In late October 1951, Local 600 took the unprecedented step of filing suit against Ford Motor Company in United States District Court before Judge Thomas P. Thornton. The lawsuit argued that Ford's attempts to decentralize production violated employees' right to work enshrined in its current contract and asked Judge Thornton to grant union workers a role in corporate economic planning. Such a request, essentially to limit the employer's freedom to hire and fire employees, challenged basic tenets of labor law. About 2,500 Rouge employees signed on to the lawsuit, but the international union, fatefully, declined to join the suit. Judge Thornton dismissed the suit, and Ford Motor Company's first steps toward decentralization would begin the unraveling of job security for Rouge employees. The leadership of UAW Local 600 was sufficiently prescient to observe that the movement of men and machines out of the Rouge plant was part of a much larger plan of Ford Motor Company to decentralize its operations. In fact, all the major auto makers started moving production to cheaper, more spacious suburban facilities. By 1957, the Big Three had built twenty-five new plants throughout suburban Detroit, including Livonia, Plymouth and Wixom to the west; Warren, Madison Heights and Sterling Heights to the north; Romulus and River Rouge to the south; and to surrounding counties. Workers followed the jobs, but black workers, unable to obtain housing in these suburban and exurban communities, were forced into long, difficult commutes.

Many and varied are the explanations for Detroit's gradual descent into bankruptcy, the largest such municipal bankruptcy in our nation's history. One contributing factor was the lack of industrial diversification. Detroit was—and largely remains—a single-industry town. Unlike cities such as Chicago and Pittsburgh, with their more diverse industrial base, Detroit's fate would rise or fall on the prowess of the automobile industry. Any other major industry planning to incorporate in the city of Detroit would have the daunting task of dealing with a very high-priced labor pool, particularly after the Treaty of Detroit.

Auto industry consolidation was another important factor. In the 1950s, smaller independent auto manufacturers—such as Hudson, Kaiser-Fraser, Crosley Motors, Nash-Kelvinator and Studebaker-Packard—were unable to compete with Detroit's "Big Three" of General Motors, Chrysler and Ford. The shutdown of such central city factories had a devastating impact on Detroit's neighborhoods and city tax revenues. Neighborhoods near closed plants, such as the Packard plant on the near east side, suffered severe population displacement as well as the closure of party stores, bars and restaurants that catered to these factories. Redeveloping this veritable wasteland of disused factories, boarded-up storefronts, abandoned homes and vacant, litter-strewn lots would prove beyond the means of city government, which was struggling to provide essential city services to an increasingly impoverished urban population.

The outmigration of whites to the suburbs and exurbs of Detroit, as well as the rise and recent decline in the number of black residents in the city, parallels the industrial decline of what was among the richest, most productive urban centers of the world in 1950. Such outmigration can be explained in strictly economic terms without reference to race. The redistribution of population strongly follows employment opportunities. As the Big Three disinvested in Detroit and moved factories into its suburbs and exurbs, the corresponding rise in the population of communities outside Detroit but within Wayne County, and in Oakland and Macomb Counties, continued through 1970.

The American auto industry, still centered in metropolitan Detroit, continued to dominate the international market. At no time during this period did import automobiles exceed 5.7 percent as a share of gross domestic product, nearly the same level as 1920. It took several decades for the industrial base of Europe and Asia to recover from the infrastructure

The corner of Eight Mile and Wyoming, the "Slave Market," circa 1950. *Dwight Smith.*

devastation occasioned by the Second World War. By 1970, these allies and former enemies of the United States had recovered sufficiently to mount a challenge to the supremacy of the American auto industry.

The Big Three—as well as other American manufacturing industries—failed to anticipate the nascent development of European and Japanese and later Korean auto makers, which began to build market share by producing high-quality vehicles that outperformed their American counterparts. The philosophy in the American automotive culture that had worked for decades—"If we build it, they will buy it"—no longer applied.

After the war and throughout the 1960s, suburban industrial, retail and housing developments created a large labor market for part-time, low-paying construction jobs. Vulnerable to the vagaries of factory closures and layoffs, unemployed blacks in Detroit became easy pickings for construction foremen who sought temporary workers willing to accept the most back-breaking jobs for a fraction of the regular hourly wage. One major gathering place in Detroit for black day laborers was the corner of Eight Mile and Wyoming. At any given time of day, contractors would drive by the intersection and pick and choose from among dozens of the unemployed men waiting for their number to be called. Like the old Shockoe Bottom in Richmond, Virginia, one of the largest centers of the U.S. slave trade, the intersection of Eight Mile and Wyoming became known among local building contractors as "the Slave Market."[66]

Chapter 4

BARRIERS TO EDUCATION

I was born into a very strict conservative household, and I remained sheltered for much of life until I started college. No movies, no boys, no dances. The only time I could visit Birdhurst, our neighborhood recreation center, was if there was some event that was intellectually stimulating or spiritually uplifting. Of course, none of that applied to my brothers. Even so, from a very young age I had my life mapped out, so to speak."

Sophia Ellis's parents were both from Birmingham, Alabama. Her mother, Ethel Lee Jones, a black child in the Reconstruction South, was educated wherever it was offered. In this case, it was at the 16th Street Baptist Church in Birmingham, where her family worshiped on Sundays and where, fifty years later, four black school girls were murdered in a bombing by white supremacist terrorists. Her father, Major Quincey Holley, left Alabama in 1918 in one of the many boxcars that Henry Ford sent south to collect potential workers for his factories in Detroit. His mother, Sophia, had already settled in the city some years before, at 1712 St. Aubin, in the heart of badly overcrowded Black Bottom. Major refused to work for Ford once he learned of the kind of jobs available for blacks in his factories. Instead, he found employment as a brass molder in a foundry on Jefferson Avenue. One day, while casting in brass the individual letters identifying the Detroit Free Press on its building marquee, he learned that one of his coworkers was his half-brother, Spencer. They got along so well, they agreed, because of their blood connection.

All the while, Major never forgot Ethel Lee back in Birmingham, and as soon as he could save a sufficient sum of money, he returned to the South to marry her—or, in African American parlance, to "jump the broom." Soon they were on their way back to Detroit, where he had very specific plans to purchase land with some of the money he had saved.

In 1924, he purchased adjacent lots on Roselawn Street, just south of Eight Mile road—one lot on which to build a house and the other to create their garden.

"Our house wasn't big by today's standards, only five rooms—a living room, a kitchen, my parents' bedroom, a bedroom for the boys and a bedroom for me—no bathroom. It was never a question of one person or one family building a house. It was a community effort; everyone pitched in. One person knew something about foundations, another about carpentry, another about roofing, yet another about plastering. It was never about bartering where you trade items or skills of equal value. You just contributed what you could to the project. Helping build the houses, without any help of the bank or professional builders, helped to build the community."

That first year, Major Holley Jr. came along (1924), followed by Harold Pharris (1925) and then Sophia in 1927. "I was a precocious little girl. I learned to read by three years old. Mother would give me things to read, and I developed a growing interest in science. One day, I remember my Uncle Vic and his wife came to visit. He could pass for white, and it proved useful, as he had attended the University of Michigan and attained his PhD in chemistry. He felt he had to hide the fact that his wife was black, and so they lived up on the hill overlooking the old train station, what is now the Gandy Dancer restaurant, where a number of black families lived at the time. I remember telling Uncle Vic that I too wanted to be a scientist one day. He said to me, 'Sophia, are you a bright little girl?' I said, 'Yes, I am.' 'Then if you want to be a scientist, you must prepare by learning German.' From that moment, I dedicated myself to learning German. I would listen to every German radio broadcast I could, and they were not uncommon in the days before the war. And I read every magazine or paper I could find in German. I was determined from that very young age that I would become a scientist, and I never wavered in that conviction.

"I was happy growing up, but it was difficult at times. My brothers and I dug out much of the basement with buckets. We dug through the sandy soil right down to the loam. My father would take the loamy soil we piled up and use it in our garden or for growing grass and shrubs around the house. It was so rich in humus and soil nutrients. I acquired an appreciation for what it took to make things grow."

When it was time to enroll in high school, Sophia and her mother visited Cooley High School to see a counselor and register for fall classes. They were told she could indeed enroll in the general curriculum, but she would not be allowed to take college preparatory classes. That option was out of the question for Sophia, so even though it meant considerable inconvenience as far as taking buses and walking each day, she would attend Northern High School on Woodward Avenue in Detroit. There, among perhaps thirty other black students among an enrollment of about one thousand, Sophia stood out academically. She studied German alongside many of the Jewish boys from Highland Park in her classes. She took as much science, especially biology and chemistry, as her schedule would allow. In time, *her efforts drew the attention of John Dancy, the director of the Detroit Urban League. Upon graduation, he arranged a full scholarship with no entrance exam requirement to the University of Michigan through the Student Aid Foundation of Michigan.*

"I remember my father did not want me to go to U of M. He didn't think much of higher education for women. I don't know what exactly he wanted me to do, but when my mother and father and a couple of family friends dropped me off in Ann Arbor, my father would not even let my mother give me a hug goodbye. When I attempted to register for classes and make living arrangements, they seemed stunned to discover I was black. They scrambled a bit and found a room for me at the home of Mrs. Lilley Roberts, the head of the law library, who lived with her husband on Washtenaw Avenue. When my English professor, Robert Shedd, of the Shedd Peanut Butter family, learned of my living arrangements, he immediately went to [the] administration and complained that this talented young lady, who's already been sheltered most of her life, desperately needed life experiences, and living in a room at the home of the law librarian was not going to give her those experiences. She needed to be with young ladies in a dormitory, setting with young ladies like herself, talking to each other about things that mattered at their age. They listened and they moved me into Mary Markle House on Washington Avenue, and the rest, as they say, is history."

Upon graduation from the College of Literature, Science and the Arts (LSA), Sophia enjoyed a long and fulfilling career in both education and community service. She had a

Sophia Holley Ellis, working as counselor at Girl Scout Camp, New York, circa 1950. *Sophia Holley Ellis.*

Sophia Holley Ellis, biology and German teacher at Martin Luther King High School, Detroit. *Sophia Holley Ellis.*

special calling as an educator and served as a role model to thousands of Detroit public school students who had dreams of their own. She taught horticulture, earth science and, of course, German and biology. As the first African American to study at the LSA's Biology Station, Sophia would return to U of M for master's degrees in both botany (1950) and German (1964). Retiring after a teaching career that spanned fifty-six years, she received numerous awards, including the Layton Perry Educator of the Year in 2006, awarded by the U.S. State Department. In 2009, Sophia started a scholarship fund in her name with a $25,000 contribution to help students from Detroit with financial need who are accepted by the LSA College.[67]

Sophia Holley Ellis, ninety-two, lives in Southfield, Michigan, and remains an active alumna of the University of Michigan.

The construction of Higginbotham School in 1926 was an event that generated tremendous community pride for the residents of the Eight Mile Road community. Designed by N.C. Sorenson and named after the famed Detroit architect who designed many churches and schools in Detroit, Higginbotham was a worthy successor to Birdhurst, which had fallen into disrepair and was barely operational as a community center. Now becoming part of the Detroit Public School System in a brand-new facility, Higginbotham promised local children access to a significant curriculum upgrade in a clean, safe environment in which to learn.

By the time the Birwood wall was constructed, Higginbotham enrolled 386 children. Even in her otherwise pointedly critical report on the West Eight Mile community, "Be It Ever So Tumbled," Marvel Daines could only make positive comments about Higginbotham: "In spite of their environment, the children in this area appear to be normal, healthy and vigorous. They are fortunate in having an excellent school with a principal who understands their problems and how best to handle them, and a fine staff of teachers, both Negro and white."[68]

The white school principal, Mr. Stemmelen, presided over a racially integrated staff and described the students as respectful and well groomed:

> *We have no delinquency problem to speak of in this area and no moral problem. Down in the congested slum area* [Black Bottom], *a child's dwelling might be in the same building with a beer garden, headquarters for a petty vice ring, or across from an establishment of ill repute. They have real problems to deal with there—juvenile delinquency, court cases, probation cases. But out here the area is entirely residential—children are not subjected to these conditions. We rarely have a case of juvenile delinquency or a case where a child must go to court.*[69]

Ranked in the middle with respect to test scores, Higginbotham enjoyed one of the highest attendance records in the entire school district. The school was especially proud of one student who had recently won the district spelling bee.

The growth of the African American community in Detroit was perhaps the single most significant demographic change brought about by the Second World War. The 1940s witnessed a doubling of the black population in Detroit, from 149,119 to 303,721. The established black neighborhoods bordering Woodward Avenue during the Great Depression expanded to include much of the central, southeastern and southwestern portions

Higginbotham School, Detroit. *Author's collection.*

of Detroit. As blacks migrated from the central city, white working-class families gravitated toward the northeastern and northwestern sections. Many of the newer families, black and white, were recent migrants from the South seeking the same thing, good jobs in the aptly dubbed "Arsenal of Democracy." These migratory patterns within the city had resulted in a highly segregated racial geography that would soon have significant political implications.

The West Eight Mile community would be in the center of three important educational and political issues facing Detroit in the decades following the Second World War: segregated schools, the decline in student achievement and the struggle to form a community college district within Wayne County.

RACIAL SEGREGATION AT GEORGE WASHINGTON CARVER ELEMENTARY SCHOOL IN ROYAL OAK TOWNSHIP

Before the substantial influx of blacks to the southern border of Oakland County, Royal Oak Township had been served by the Clinton School District. As blacks began settling both sides of Eight Mile in large numbers during World War II, school administrators, fearing racial disharmony if its schools were allowed to become fully integrated, divided the larger district into two racially segregated districts. African American children would attend school within the newly constituted Carver District, named after George Washington Carver, the revered African American botanist and inventor. With the help of federal funding, a new George Washington Carver Elementary School was planned to be built on property on Mendota Street, just west of Wyoming; it would be completed in time to greet its first K–8 grade school children in September 1945. Meanwhile, children would attend the old Wineman School, a one-room schoolhouse across the street, which had been part of the Clinton School District No. 3 formed in 1922. The new Carver District added a two-room portable classroom to absorb the overflow of arriving students.[70]

Recognizing after the war that the school district's tax base was insufficient to fund the construction of or maintain its own high school, the district reached out unsuccessfully to neighboring school districts to absorb its Carver graduates. After much negotiation, the district agreed to terms with the Detroit Public Schools (DPS) whereby in exchange for tuition payments, Carver graduates would be bused to and attend classes at Northern High School, a largely black high school on Woodward Avenue.

In 1959, the Carver School District fell behind in meeting tuition obligations to the Detroit Public Schools, owing in excess of $125,000 in back payments. Decreased tax revenues, coupled with corruption and mismanagement of funds, made it impossible for the district to meet its obligations. In June, the DPS informed the Carver School Board that after June 1960 it would no longer accept tuition students. This was prompted by the large Carver school debt, overcrowded conditions in the Detroit schools and, importantly, criticisms by the Citizens Committee for Better Schools. This all–African American committee questioned the segregation pattern of busing Carver district students nearly eight miles into a school in Detroit. There was little immediate action taken by the Carver School Board to seek a solution. However, a survey of the sixty-seven graduating eighth graders in June revealed that only twenty-four were still in the district. The remaining forty-three had either moved out of the district or were planning to by the end of the summer.[71]

The most apparent impediment to a solution was the financial responsibility placed on any district accepting the Carver School District. A substantial tuition payment debt to the DPS existed, and additional costs were evident to upgrade the school and assume eventual responsibility for

Carver Elementary School, Royal Oak Township. *Author's collection.*

Northern High School, Woodward and Clairmont, 1935. *Walter P. Reuther Library, Archives of Labor and Urban Affairs, Wayne State University.*

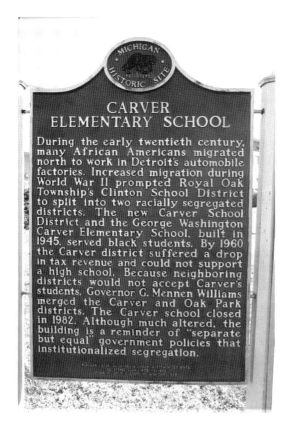

Carver Elementary School
historical marker. *Author's collection.*

several hundred high school youth. Any district that became concerned with the area in which the students lived had to recognize the additional needs for adult education, recreation, health and special school services. This impediment seemed so formidable that all other basic concerns were cloaked in this problem. Some residents were hoping and expecting that this problem would be financially too great to assume and would thus obviate their responsibility. Others had fears and doubts on class or social lines. Race was perhaps uppermost of the impediments to a solution, although this was not primarily or openly emphasized. It had a way of permeating the entire issue without a race label.

A Citizens Committee in Oak Park and several human relations agencies, active in the community, played significant organizational roles. The Young Democrats and the Liberal-Labor Caucus of the senior Oakland County Democratic Party were involved to act as strong influences that could reach the governor's office. Petitions were circulated in Oak Park (as well as counter petitions) and support elicited from Royal Oak Township residents to reach a solution for September. The Republican county chairman suggested that Oak Park, Ferndale and the DPS each take some of the twenty-four students to meet the immediate problem. One of the principal means of applying pressure for a solution was through publicity. A key article was arranged in *TIME* magazine early in September through the Anti-Defamation League of Detroit. The September 5, 1960 *TIME* article "The Unwanted" sparked added coverage in the *Detroit News* and *Detroit Free Press*, Detroit's two major metropolitan dailies, and was a key spur to the governor's personal involvement in effecting a solution. As a stopgap measure, the district established a one-room high school within Carver Elementary.

As media attention further intensified, Governor G. Mennan Williams suggested the dissolution of the Carver School District and attachment to a neighboring district by the Oakland County Board of Education. After the governor's efforts, three of five school board members resigned immediately, the remaining two under pressure. After the resignations, the County Board of Education set a special election to fill the vacated school board positions as required by law. If no school board member were elected, the County Board of Education would be required to attach Carver to another district immediately.

Dissolution was the only answer left, yet it depended on the Carver School District citizens *not* to elect (that is, refuse to elect) anyone to the board. Following the election, when no candidates registered and no ballots were cast, the Oak Park and Ferndale School Districts declared their unwillingness to accept responsibility for the district, either entirely or conditionally. The Ferndale School Board said it had fulfilled its obligations by providing high school facilities for about half of the Royal Oak Township area that was not part of the Carver District. After this, the Oak Park School Board wanted to settle for a split between itself and Ferndale, with additional financial aid from the county and state. However, it was officially announced by the Oakland County Board of Education to assign the district to Oak Park. The attachment of the Carver School to the Oak Park School District was the only expedient remedy open to the county board. Yet this decision did not help to unite the Royal Oak Township area into one cohesive unit. With two separate school districts, organization of recreation, health, adult education and special school services had to continue on a divided basis. One school district's services seldom tied with that of the neighboring school district, thus adding a strong need for joint effort and coordination.[72]

Consolidation with Oak Park Schools led to changes at Carver Elementary. A large part of the facility was sold to Royal Oak Township for one dollar to be used as both a recreational facility and a library. The remaining portion of the building would continue to be used as an elementary school. By 1982, however, continued consolidation and ongoing costs of repair had made its use as an educational facility problematic. Currently, it serves as the township's recreation center, and the library was moved to the second floor of the Township Administrative Building on Garden Lane.

"My parents brought me north from Mississippi in 1944 when I was ten years old. They came to find work in the factories during the war. We settled in one of the one-story projects just north of Eight Mile Road in Royal Oak Township."

Growing up, Gloria Butler remembers having to stay warm in the winter around a potbellied stove in the kitchen. They would feed it coal or wood from a bin kept just outside the door. Her mother was able to secure a job at Chrysler, she recalled, but her father, a skilled carpenter, had a difficult time because African Americans were excluded from the skilled trade unions and the higher wages and benefits that went with them.

Gloria attended school at the racially segregated Carver Elementary School on Mendota Street. The new school was not ready in 1944, so she attended Wineman, taking all her classes in the two-room portable that had been added until construction on the new building was completed. After graduating, she and her classmates had few options since the neighboring city of Ferndale would not accept them at Lincoln High School, even though it was just up the road at Livernois and Nine Mile Road. In an arrangement with Detroit Public Schools, Gloria and her friends were bused every morning from Carver Elementary to Northern High School on Woodward Avenue. She attended Northern for four years, graduating in 1953.

"The first year I was at Northern, I would have to get up extra early in the morning because I would have to take public transportation to get to Northern in downtown Detroit. My dad would give me a ride to the fairgrounds, where I would catch the streetcar going south on Woodward. The next year, arrangements were made whereby we were picked up at Carver in DSR buses and taken directly to Northern. The problem was that the buses to return home left sharply at 3:00 p.m., so we couldn't really participate in any extracurricular after-school activities. In 1950, I think it was, the DSR went on strike for about three months. What a mess. We wound up carpooling and hitch-hiking to get to and from school. Still, overall, I liked it at Northern. I made friends; the school was still mixed race. I had friends. In my classes, there were Jews and Gentiles, and all my teachers were white. Over time, it started turning more and more black."

The family would move to the Detroit side of Eight Mile Road before the Royal Oak Township wartime projects were torn down to make way for new development.

Gloria Butler, celebrating high school graduation from Northern High School, 1952. *Gloria Butler.*

"Despite the hardships and discrimination we experienced—especially when we stepped outside our safe zone—my friends and I in the projects adapted and lived our lives. We went to the Duke to watch the Saturday serials for twenty-five cents. They used to have live talent shows, and when I got older, bands that would regularly play at the Paradise downtown would come up and play at the Duke—bands like Todd Rose, Paul Williams

and L'il Willie John. We'd have street parties in the projects and skate over at Carver. Just off Eight Mile Road, there was a small strip of stores running north and south that took care of most of our needs, so we didn't have to venture very far out of the township. Next to the Duke was a 5 and 10 and a Cunningham's Drug Store. There was Buddy's Record Shop and an A&P grocery store. Right next door to each other, a little farther down, was Loretta's Beauty Parlor and Stan's Barber Shop. And right next to Vickie's BBQ, my mom and I used to go to a place that had live chickens and fish. You'd pick out the chicken, they'd slaughter and dress it right there for you. I guess we had just about everything we needed to get by in those days."

Gloria Butler, eighty-four, and her son, Keith, reside presently in a modest, well-maintained brick bungalow on Cherrylawn, directly across the street from the Johnson Recreation Center and Joe Louis Field.[73]

RACIAL SEGREGATION AT GRANT ELEMENTARY SCHOOL IN ROYAL OAK TOWNSHIP

While Carver Elementary served the western portion of the township, Ferndale School district's Grant Elementary School served the area east of Wyoming. In its very early days, the village of Ferndale grew exponentially. In 1920, the village reported 2,640 residents. During the following ten years, Ferndale grew by 690 percent, reporting 20,855 residents by 1930. Even before it incorporated as a city in 1927, Ferndale had difficulty keeping up with the baby boom and its impact on existing school facilities. From 1920 to 1926, Ferndale built seven new elementary schools: Harding (1920), Roosevelt (1920), Washington (1923), Wilson (1923), Coolidge (1925), Jefferson (1925) and Grant (1926). One year before construction was completed on Grant Elementary School, the Ferndale School District authorized a Neighborhood Schools Plan whereby children would be selected to attend the school closest to home, ideally within half a mile. Restrictive covenants sewn into the fabric of property deeds at the time ensured that the population just east of Wyoming along Eight Mile Road would remain almost exclusively black.

The nice and neat packaging of students along racial lines was disrupted by the special situation at Jefferson Elementary School. As a direct result of the Neighborhood Schools Plan, 101 black students (or 34 percent of school enrollment) fell within the half mile radius of Jefferson Elementary; 196 white students from the southwest portion of Ferndale made up the balance of enrollment. While it is unclear if a particular threshold had been crossed with respect to an acceptable number of black students enrolled in a district school (for example, would there have even been an issue if only 3 black students were enrolled?), the school board, citing specific disturbances at the school, declared Grant Elementary no longer autonomous but to now function as an ancillary of Jefferson School, with Jefferson's principal to remain in his position while overseeing Grant. Furthermore, the board proceeded to gerrymander school boundaries for Grant students that included only black neighborhoods east of Wyoming, including the Forest Grove and Detroyal subdivisions.[74]

African American parents of Jefferson Elementary School children had little reason to believe that the Ferndale School Board was acting in their children's best interests, particularly after the board cynically hired African American teachers whose teaching duties were restricted solely to Grant Elementary School until 1949; conversely, no white teachers or staff were hired, transferred or permitted to work at Grant until 1952. Segregating fully credentialed teachers on the basis of race alone creates yet another dimension of racial discrimination, implying at least that students would or could not receive the same quality education because of race.

For several years after the Jefferson Elementary debacle, the overcrowded conditions at Grant remained unrelieved despite the fact that Jefferson and other area schools had excess capacity. The excuse used, that turmoil and disharmony would naturally follow from integration, was simply providing cover for the long-standing legal doctrine established in *Plessy v. Ferguson* of "separate but equal," which would not be overturned until 1954 in *Brown v. Board of Education.*

Ernest Wilson, chairman of the Equal Opportunity in Education Committee, expressed concern that the children in the district were not receiving the benefits of integration, namely that regular social interaction and direct communication between black and white children would foster mutual understanding and break down barriers that segregation imposes and perpetuates. Since the board refused to consider redrawing school boundaries, Wilson petitioned the United States Department of Health, Education and Welfare to investigate the Ferndale School District for potential violations of the Civil Rights Act of 1964. From 1968 to 1974, the Ferndale School District remained in litigation with the federal government over the issue of whether federal funds to the school district should be withheld for its violations of the Civil Rights Act. Ferndale School District thus became the first northern school district to be cited for such violations. Throughout the legal proceedings, Ferndale maintained that at no time was

Grant Elementary School, Royal Oak Township. *Author's collection.*

Grant School class photo, 1940s. *John Gatewood.*

there a deliberate attempt to segregate students racially at any school and that Grant Elementary was African American simply because of the racial makeup of its immediate neighborhood.[75]

In 1975, the school district began the voluntary implementation of programs designed to mitigate damages imposed on children by de facto (rather than deliberate, or de jure) segregation. First, the school board permitted, even encouraged, Grant Elementary School children to enroll in any Ferndale public elementary school. Second, the board introduced an open classroom program at grant, available to any student in any of its schools; the program offered individualized attention in a flexible learning environment. However, following the programs' mixed results, the United States Department of Justice took the formal position that these programs were "too little, too late" and sought a federal court order to integrate schools within the Ferndale School District. The Federal District Court in Detroit issued an order, which was confirmed by the Sixth Circuit Court of Appeals in 1980, to integrate Grant Elementary School with two other elementary schools within the district. It would take fifteen more years before the same Federal District Court lifted monitoring.

When my family moved to Ferndale in 1955, housing segregation was the norm. Ferndale and Royal Oak were white, Royal Oak Township was black and Detroit was mixed and in the process of transition from majority-white to majority-black. The segregation in housing resulted in the segregation of public schools, since the boundaries of school districts were aligned with the boundaries of cities. Few, if any, businesses in Ferndale had black employees. So, in addition to interactions with neighbors, socializing with friends, and attending school, shopping at stores was also an all-white experience.

As kids in elementary school, we rarely if ever thought about the issue of race. Interacting with other white people was the norm. We did not notice a lack of black people in our daily life. But people did notice, and often commented on, the occasional black face in an otherwise all-white suburban world.

I do not recall any teacher at school—whether in social science, civics or government classes—or any adult family members ever mentioning the significance of the 1948 Supreme Court case of Shelly v. Kramer. *That landmark decision prohibited courts from enforcing restrictive covenants that prohibited racial minorities from buying property in white communities. The communities stayed white because these contracts, forced on everyone who would buy land, prohibited them from ever selling to a member of the Negro race. These covenants had contributed to cities in Oakland County, such as Ferndale, staying all white. Despite the Supreme Court's edict, it took two decades or more for implied agreements among neighbors to give way to nondiscrimination in housing transactions.*

I also do not recall any discussion at school, or at home, about the 1954 court decision in Brown v. Board of Education—*a ruling by the United States Supreme Court that prohibited racial segregation in public schools and paved the way for integration. I was probably out playing in the park when the nightly television news carried a story in 1957 about federal soldiers forcing a school in Arkansas to admit black students. At the time, the issue of racial integration of the schools was not discussed in our house—at least I don't remember any such conversations by my parents.*

The only place that my friends and I would occasionally cross paths with black people was at the Top Hat hamburger joint at the corner of Eight Mile Road and Livernois which was about three blocks from our house. Although it was in Ferndale, it was at a main intersection south of which there was a growing black population.

Since I was not into sports, I did not have any interest to play basketball on the newly erected "magic square" in Taft Park across the street from our house. It was a multi-purpose concrete area that was used for impromptu basketball games for young men in the summer, ice skating for boys and girls and adults in the winter, and square dancing for older adults during evenings in warm weather months.

The hoops attracted young black men from across Eight Mile Road who lacked nice basketball courts where they lived. So they crossed the "racial divide" and ventured into white territory to play a game or two of basketball. I do recall hearing words of disdain from people in our neighborhood who expressed their feelings that the young men should "stay on their own side."

Although the problems of racial discrimination and anti-Semitism existed back then, my grade school days were mostly focused on learning in school, praying in church, chores, homework, playing with friends, watching television, going to the movies, and listening to my transistor radio.[76]

Thomas Coleman currently lives in California.

RACIAL POLITICS AT HIGGINBOTHAM SCHOOL

In the fall of 1947, a conflict between Higginbotham School parents and the Detroit Board of Education became one of the first major tests of district policy over the issue of school segregation. School district administrators reassigned all of the black seventh- and eighth-grade students at Loren M. Post Intermediate School to Higginbotham. School Superintendent Arthur Dondineau explained that the transfer was necessary to avoid half-day sessions because of a classroom shortage. What Higginbotham parents found particularly galling, however, was the reopening of Birdhurst to accommodate the overflow of students at Higginbotham. Seen as evidence of an emerging "separate but equal" school system, representatives of Carver Progressive Club and the Detroit branch of the NAACP denounced the transfer as blatantly segregationist.

The Detroit School Board refused to reconsider the reassignments, so in response, parents pulled their children from Higginbotham and Birdhurst and established picket lines around both schools. For almost two weeks, "not one child between the first and eighth grades attended" either school, reported the *Detroit Tribune*.[77]

In a meeting called by Superintendent Dondineau to defuse the situation, things deteriorated quickly. Parents and members of both the Carver Progressive Club and the NAACP repeated their demands for the district to reverse its reassignment decision and even accused Dondineau of blatant racial discrimination. In retaliation, the superintendent threatened parents with court action if they did not immediately return their children to school. Outraged over being threatened, the parents yelled, "There's not enough jails in the state to hold all parents who will keep their children out of school."[78]

One week later, with the parents showing no signs of wavering, Dondineau struck a more conciliatory tone in a second meeting. He agreed to shutter Birdhurst, renovate Higginbotham to accommodate the influx of new students and establish a committee to study the issue of segregation within the school district. While parents failed to get everything they initially demanded, they nonetheless declared victory and sent their children off to Higginbotham.

The same year, the Citizens Committee for Better Schools, a liberal education advocacy group, issued a stern rebuke of Arthur Dondineau in the form of a press release directly attributing the school district's current financial plight and overcrowded classes to eight years of mismanagement. The significance of the press release is who signed it: seventeen liberal and civil rights organizations, including the Carver Progressive Club, which had organized the Higginbotham-Birdhurst strike, and the Higginbotham PTA. Eight Mile and Wyoming parents were finding a voice—an important, progressive voice on behalf of the children of the city of Detroit; no longer were their interests purely parochial. The press release established what would become widely known over the next quarter century as the "liberal-labor-black coalition," which would grow to have significant influence over municipal and educational policies.[79]

Twelve years later, northwest Detroit was the scene of another conflict between the school district and black parents over the issue of school integration. In early October 1959, district administrators announced plans for seventy-four black children to be transferred from badly overcrowded Patengill Elementary School to Houghton Elementary, four miles away. The crux of the issue for the Patengill parents was that administrators had bypassed two predominantly white elementary schools with sufficient capacity to absorb the seventy-four black children. Inspired by the actions taken by black parents during the Higginbotham-Birdhurst controversy, parents boycotted Pattengill School and refused to allow their children to board the buses for Houghton.[80] This action drew the attention of Samuel Brownell, who had replaced Arthur Dondineau following his resignation in October 1955. Brownell came to the appointment as former U.S. commissioner of education, an outsider acutely aware of the problems of segregated schools and the growing intolerance among black families over their continued existence. Also, unlike his predecessor, Brownell favored citizen participation in educational policy decisions. The liberal-labor-black coalition had done its homework in influencing Detroit's progressive board of education to tender the job offer to Brownell.

Instead of the kind of contentious meeting the Higginbotham parents faced with Arthur Dondineau, Brownell and the Patengill parents came to a meeting of the minds with respect to the cause of the Houghton transfer plan: it had simply been a mistake, not a deliberate strategy, and Brownell assured the parents that the problem would be rectified at the end of the semester. Board members further assured parents that policies would be put into place to avoid such occurrences again.

The Pattengill Controversy served notice to the community in general that a progressive agenda was being established by the new school administration, and that message was further confirmed by the creation, in January 1960, of the Citizens Advisory Committee on Equal Educational Opportunities (CAC-EEO), chaired by Probate Judge Nathan J. Kaufman, to investigate allegations of racial discrimination within the school system.

A significant test case faced the board and the CAC-EEO later the same year in the same northwestern section of the city—but this time by white parents protesting the busing of black students into predominantly white schools. School officials had announced plans to bus nearly three hundred black students from overcrowded central city schools to underutilized Guest, Monier and Noble schools. Parents at the three schools threatened to keep their children home when the buses of black children arrived. A newly formed organization, the Northwest Detroit Parents Committee, further threatened to recall all seven members of the school board and the rescission of any such busing plans.

A parents committee agreed to meet with Brownell and representatives of various organizations supported by the liberal-labor-black coalition. Brownell stood before an audience of nearly two thousand community members who came to witness the presentation Brownell made to the parents group to explain the evolution of busing over the past decade. The only difference, in the present instance, Brownell emphasized, was that the children were black. What amounted to a populist uprising ensued, as parents ignored all appeals from the various church and union groups in attendance to support the busing plan. Several days of boycotts ensued, but neither Brownell nor the board budged an inch. Meanwhile, the black children were bused to Guest, Monier and Noble without further incident, in no small part owing to the police presence for a sustained period.

The integration of the three schools proved a hollow victory for administration, as a decision was made, possibly as a backdoor concession to the still irate white parents, to segregate the three hundred black children within all three schools.

The liberal-labor-black coalition had made significant strides during the 1950s and 1960s in its commitment to racial equality, illustrated in the hiring of large numbers of black teachers, in the major construction projects within black neighborhoods and in the series of nondiscrimination resolutions adopted by the board of education. By the mid-1960s, however, more aggressive black and white constituencies would be demanding more permanent solutions to the issue of desegregation in Detroit schools.

Perhaps the greatest opportunity to begin to resolve the issue of racial segregation came in a series of court decisions in the early 1970s within the Detroit Public School System. Had these court cases led to a different resolution, ultimately by the United States Supreme Court in *Milliken v. Bradley*, a plan to integrate Detroit schools by reaching beyond the city's limits to include white students in the suburbs would have been approved and the historic nexus between segregated schools and discriminatory real estate practices would have been acknowledged by the highest court in the land, with implications for metropolitan areas across the country.

Years earlier, the United States Supreme Court had overturned *Plessy v. Ferguson*, which had upheld the "separate but equal" doctrine, derived originally from an 1890 Louisiana law. The high court's 1954 ruling in *Brown v. Topeka Board of Education* provided the constitutional basis for overturning the de jure racial segregation in schools of the South. However, northern schools like Detroit's managed to evade the reach of *Brown* by engaging in a form of de facto racial segregation that appeared on the surface to simply be the product of free choice and happenstance.

On August 18, 1970, three years after the Twelfth Street Riot, the NAACP filed suit in federal district court to redress policies and practices that resulted in the racial segregation of Detroit schools. In a forty-one-day trial beginning April 6, 1971, in the courtroom of Judge Stephen J. Roth, the NAACP presented expert witnesses who provided compelling evidence that African Americans were the victims of a clear historic conspiracy to create a racially segregated housing market in Detroit and its suburbs and that segregated schools were an unavoidable consequence. The FHA and VA policies of restrictive residential covenants, as well as the coordinated practices of local banks and real estate brokers, all contributed to keeping black children in black schools located in black neighborhoods within the city of Detroit.[81]

In September 1971, Judge Roth issued a ruling that sent shock waves throughout Detroit and threatened to destabilize the entire metropolitan region. Finding housing and school segregation essentially interdependent and perpetuated by egregious policies of the Detroit School Board, the State of Michigan and its various agencies, Judge Roth directed the Detroit Board of Education to submit a cross-district busing desegregation plan. In June of the following year, the board presented an inter-district remedy that involved fifty-three metropolitan school districts. The goal of the remedy was not only to integrate Detroit schools but to discourage further white flight. Had the ruling been restricted to enforcing busing solely within the city of Detroit, the cure would have been worse that the disease: middle-class whites would more than likely have fled to the suburbs rather than permit their children to be bused across town.

On appeal, the Sixth Circuit affirmed Roth's remedy, based on discriminatory school policies, but chose not to address the issue of interdependence between housing discrimination and school segregation. Furthermore, owing to a technical defect in the Roth directive, the appeals court prohibited the state from purchasing 295 buses to effect the implementation of the inter-district busing plan.

Meanwhile, the State of Michigan and the affected Detroit suburbs jointly appealed to the United States Supreme Court. Arguing that the suburban communities had formed no policies that discriminated against black children—ironically, housing policies made *that* unnecessary—the high court reversed the decision of the appeals court and remanded the case to the district court to devise and implement a Detroit-only solution to segregation.

DECLINING ACADEMIC ACHIEVEMENT

Community engagement was a critical factor in the decision to hire Samuel Brownell as the new superintendent of Detroit Public Schools. Rejecting the corporate, closed-door mentality of his predecessor, Brownell immediately set about addressing the major issues confronting the district. To this end, he created the Citizens' Advisory Committee on School Needs (CAC). George Romney, president of American Motors, agreed to chair the committee, which was specifically tasked to investigate five areas of the school system—curriculum, personnel, buildings, community relations and finance—and then make recommendations for policy and programmatic change.

Eighteen months after the CAC accepted its mandate, Romney reported the results of the investigation in a speech before the Economic Club of Detroit. As expected, the investigation turned up significant shortcomings: overcrowded and decaying schools, a severe shortage of qualified teachers and inadequate curricular offerings in a number of areas. It was in regard to the curriculum that the committee made its most critical misjudgment. True, it had correctly called for reform in the quantity and quality of course offerings in mathematics, science and foreign language. Yet it failed to address the issue of general track consignment that had poorly prepared a large number of otherwise capable black students to pursue higher education. Black students were routinely counseled into such coursework as childcare, hygiene, health, physical education and occupational information. The rationale—established decades earlier but now being reaffirmed by the CAC—postulated that such "practical" education would not only prepare general track students for semi-skilled and unskilled employment opportunities but also stem the high dropout rate and juvenile delinquency. Detroit high schools—particularly ones predominantly black with large numbers of general track students—had become custodial institutions preparing them for jobs that no longer existed. In a few years' time, the failure to address the problems associated with general tracking would create a public relations nightmare for the board of education and a tragedy for a generation of students.

In October 1966, the district office released standardized test results for each school in the district. Higginbotham School students were eighteen months to two years below the national norms. Outraged, Higginbotham parents threatened to boycott the school until the issue was satisfactorily addressed. However, earlier the same year, an incident at Northern High

School should have set off alarm bells well before the release of the standardized test results.[82]

In late March, twelfth-grade honor student Charles Colding penned an editorial entitled "Educational Camouflage" for his high school newspaper, the *Northern Light*. In retrospect, the academic issues Colding and others were attempting to highlight were painfully obvious. In Professor Sidney Fine's analysis:

> *More than 98 percent of its twenty-three hundred students as of 1966 were black, and most did not appear to be making very much academic progress. In a 1965–66 test of randomly selected ninth grade students, 55.5 percent of Northern's ninth graders scored below the sixth grade level in reading ability. On a February 1965 educational progress test given 10B and 12B students, seventy-six percent of the tested Northern students scored below average in math, seventy-eight percent in science, and seventy-nine percent in reading. Only about twenty percent of the class scheduled to graduate in June 1966 had achieved a twelfth grade academic level.[83]*

Contrasted with the attainment of students at predominantly white schools like Redford High School, Colding decried the policy of social promotion and the failure of segregated black schools to prepare for the real world or for the rigors of college.

Just outside the educational quality debate being waged by an increasing number of students, parents and local activists was the inner-city political scene at that time. Like Harlem and Oakland, California, Detroit was a hotbed of civil rights activism. The Detroit branch of the NAACP, the largest in the United States with eighteen thousand members, was the least militant of such organizations operating in Detroit. Within its segregated communities, the voices of the more radical groups such as Black Christian Nationalism, the Republic of New Afrika, Uhuru and the League of Revolutionary Black Workers—all founded by Detroiters—would undoubtedly have been heard by youngsters coming of age during this volatile period.[84] And so, while Superintendent Brownell was debating with board members what to do at Northern, students were compiling a laundry list of grievances, not the least of which was the immediate removal of Principal Arthur Carty, who they claimed was antagonistic to their demands, and Bonnie Lucas, the black policeman assigned to Northern, who was accused of harassment and intimidation.

Students returned from Easter break on April 18, only to find that things hadn't much changed. While some students proceeded to meet their classes, the majority congregated across the street at St. Joseph's Church to set up a Freedom School, staffed by volunteer professors from Wayne State University. News of the boycott saturated the daily newspapers, and before students eventually voted to end their boycott the following week, the community had become polarized. Local citizenry, particularly in the white neighborhoods, shared a sense of outrage with a number of school administrators, who felt that Brownell had caved in order to end the boycott. Carty was out as principal, and a host of issues was now being addressed by the Northern High School Study committee. On May 9, the voters would formally express their opinions at the polling precincts. The results were not unexpected under the circumstances. The 2.5 mill tax levy urgently needed by the Detroit Public Schools failed by a voted of 79,746 to 67,815, or 54 to 46 percent of the vote.[85]

THE STRUGGLE TO FIND ACCESSIBLE, AFFORDABLE POSTSECONDARY EDUCATION AND TRAINING

Also in 1966, efforts to organize a community college to serve the needs of metropolitan Detroit surprisingly failed despite a very well-organized and well-financed campaign. Residents in Northwest Detroit, particularly in the working-class neighborhoods of West Eight Mile Road, were in dire need of accessible, affordable postsecondary education and job training for employment, particularly after the fiasco at Northern High School earlier in the year revealed how ill-prepared many black student graduates were for the real world of employment.

At this time, Wayne County was the largest metropolitan region in the United States without a coordinated community college system. In a single thirty-six-month period, four counties either bordering or very near Detroit established community colleges: Macomb (1963), Monroe (1964), Oakland (1964) and Washtenaw (1965). Ironically, the establishment of these community colleges within such a brief period did not produce the complete domino effect anticipated.

There were several factors mitigating the establishment of a community college in Wayne County. First of all, existing institutions in and around Detroit steadily absorbed students from outside their immediate service district. For students in northwest Detroit who had reliable transportation and could afford the expensive, out-of-district tuition rates, Oakland Community College was an option. For students in northeast Detroit—that is, in the neighborhoods east of Woodward Avenue—Macomb Community College's location at Lincoln High School in Warren was a possibility. On Detroit's southern border, Henry Ford Community College was a third option. In 1952, trustees of the Henry Ford Trade School voted to disband the school and transfer $1 million in assets to the school board to form a community college that would offer vocational and technical training. A degree in technical education not heretofore available in the area drew the support of local business and industry and made the college a regional magnet. A gift of seventy-five prime acres of real estate from the Henry Ford Fairlane estate allowed the college to erect seven new buildings and offer a comprehensive range of programs so attractive that nonresidents were willing to pay nearly double the resident tuition rate to attend.

Finally, in the center of Detroit, in the municipal enclave of Highland Park, Highland Park Community College (HPCC) continued to serve not only its shrinking body of district constituents but also, increasingly, students from Detroit. Ever since Henry Ford moved offices and operations out of Highland Park and into Dearborn, both the city's population and its tax base began to gradually decline. In order to compensate for the revenue decline, HPCC began to market its services beyond municipal boundaries. In the decade following World War II, for example, HPCC established a marketing radius of about twenty miles. During the period of expanded outreach, nonresident enrollment surged, from 58.9 percent in 1945 to 85.3 percent in 1954. By 1966, African Americans constituted nearly half of the college's enrollment. In the years following Wayne County Community College's establishment, HPCC's enrollment, physical plant and revenue stream steadily deteriorated, resulting in closure in 1996. HPCC had fulfilled its mission admirably for seventy-eight years, first as a junior college from 1918 to 1962 and then as a community college from 1962 until the time of its closure.[86]

Yet another major factor in delaying the establishment of a community college centered in Detroit was suburban isolationism. The first and second ring suburbs encircling Detroit were neutral at best and hostile at worst over the suggestion of joining Detroit in developing a low-cost, easily accessible multi-campus system serving Detroit and its close-in suburbs.

As early as 1957, the extreme northwestern section of Wayne County began efforts to form a separate college district centered in Livonia. Under the leadership of Benton Yates, an executive committee was formed and drew from Plymouth, Clarenceville, Garden City, Redford Union and South Redford. Professor Raymond J. Young, of the University of Michigan's Bureau of School services, was engaged by the committee to determine what college programs would fit the specific needs of the community. However, differentiating these needs from the service district of Henry Ford Community College and the far west side of Detroit, whose city limit was less than two miles from the easternmost edge of Livonia, was quite problematic. In February 1961, the Citizens' Survey Committee and the University of Michigan published its report, highlighting "sufficient enrollment prospects, unmet educational needs, financial resources, available site locations, and evidence of progressive community interest and willingness to support social and civic enterprises to warrant the establishment of a community college." In all the boilerplate language of the report, no mention is made of the city of Detroit. Four months later, voters in two of the participating districts, Redford Union and South Redford, rejected the establishment. Thus, by law, the proposal was defeated. A second, successful election was held the following October in the four supportive districts: Livonia, Clarenceville, Plymouth and Garden City. Northville would later join the new multi-district community college. Northwest Wayne County Community College was established in 1961. Early in 1963, the college changed its name to Schoolcraft College, omitting "Community" so that its abbreviation would not create the erroneous impression that the school was located in Schoolcraft County in Michigan's Upper Peninsula.

Efforts in Wyandotte to organize a Downriver Community College—separate and apart from any working relationship or sharing of resources with the city of Detroit—did not fare as well. As early as 1956, Wyandotte School superintendent Peter Jenema had been intrigued by the idea of establishing a community college in the oldest and largest city in Wayne County's downriver community. However, a series of public acts in 1959 and 1960 made it more economically sound to join with other nearby communities to form a multi-district organization. To this end, Jenema called a meeting of suburban downriver school districts—including Gibraltar, Grosse Ile, Heintzen, Riverview, Southgate and Trenton—for the purpose of discussing a jointly administered community college. Curiously, the two downriver districts with sizable African American populations, River Rouge and Ecorse, were not invited to the meeting.

With the exception of local newspaper coverage, specifically the *Wyandotte News-Herald* and the *Wyandotte Tribune*, the general public was largely shut out of the decision-making process. Instead of a "Citizen's Study," any analysis or recommendations to be produced came from the school district superintendents working in cohort. As the December 19, 1960 establishment vote drew near, the respective newspaper editorials, news stories and letters to the editor became the chief means by which the general public stayed informed on the issues. The *News-Herald* had supported the idea of a community college since its earliest articulation. Press releases from the superintendent's offices reported the endorsements of the three major state universities, as well as of the state's largest Catholic university, the University of Detroit. As late as December 18, a day before the election, there was little reason for the superintendents to believe that the establishment election was no more than a formality, or so even the *Detroit News* believed.[87]

However, the much smaller *Wyandotte Tribune* waged an aggressive counterattack on the assumptions underlying the establishment proposal. The paper questioned, for instance, the support of the University of Detroit, producing a letter from President Lawrence Britt calling into question the efficacy of the community college mission; moreover, a letter from one of the university's most outspoken professors and downriver residents, Peter J. Stanlis, PhD, suggested that a downriver branch of the University of Michigan similar to those in Flint and Dearborn would be a much more appropriate alternative to a community college.[88] Even Russell Kirk, the *National Review*'s conservative firebrand, weighed in on this local issue by suggesting that the proposal was little more than another educational boondoggle.[89] Finally, the Wyandotte Chemical Corporation, a major local employer and the city's largest private property owner, railed against the increased tax burden a community college would impose on the citizenry.[90]

The defeat of the proposal on December 19 left proponents stunned, unable to account for the fact that three of five districts—including Wyandotte, the epicenter of the movement—voted the measure down. While the downriver measure failed, by a significant margin, efforts to revive in subsequent years continued apace, and many years later, long after WCCCD was operating as a county-wide system of five campuses, a secessionist movement originated in the downriver community.

The failure of the downriver campaign, coupled with the success of the Schoolcraft College campaign, served only to galvanize proponents of a county-wide community college before the rest of Detroit's suburbs—and their substantial tax base—splintered off into separate community college districts.

The 1966 establishment campaign failed for several reasons. One was the nature and complexity of the ballot. Voters would have to approve or reject two proposals simultaneously, an establishment proposal and a tax levy proposal, and according to state law, the two proposals would be interdependent—in other words, for one to pass, both would have to pass. Another reason for the failure of the establishment campaign was the fact that on the same ballot, the Detroit Public Schools was asking city residents for a 2.5 mill property tax boost to ease them out of another financial crisis brought on by the usual suspects—industrial flight, white flight and property tax flight. Detroit homeowners were especially tax weary following Mayor Jerry Cavanagh's 1 percent income tax imposition on residents and 0.5 percent on nonresident city workers just a few years before. And now homeowners were being asked to shoulder the burden of both a failing school system and a vaguely perceived postsecondary institution. Another reason for the establishment failure was the impact of the Northern High School fiasco during the early spring. For many months thereafter, the story line would divide residents in both the city and its suburbs along racial lines.

In 1967, several state legislators were at work on a legislative solution to the community college issue. The solution would include a single, county-wide district in which an elected board of trustees would be granted the authority to levy a subsistence property tax millage without the vote of the electorate. On July 18, the bill was sent to Governor Romney's office for his signature. Before he could schedule the official signing into law, however, all hell broke loose at the intersection of Twelfth Street and Clairmount Avenue in Detroit's near west side in the early morning hours of Sunday, July 23. For the remainder of July, all attention—local, state and national—would be focused on the chaos unfolding in the streets of Mayor Jerry Cavanagh's "Model City." On August 12, 1967, after much of the smoke had cleared and once order was restored in Detroit, Governor Romney was able to direct his attention to legislative matters. With his office full of state legislators, he signed the bill that would establish Wayne County Community College, and a new chapter in postsecondary education was to be written for the residents of Wayne County.

A quarter century would pass before the first voter-approved millage would put the college on solid financial footing. In November 1992, voters approved a permanent 1 mill property tax assessment by the narrowest of margins: 263,541 yea, 261,447 nay, or 50.19 percent to 49.8 percent. A mere 2,064 votes separated victory from disaster as the state was preparing to phase out its line-item subsidy to the college over a five-year period.

A noteworthy transformation occurred in 2008 at the Northwest Campus, which serves the West Eight Mile community and is the center for WCCCD's nursing and allied health programs. The Greenfield Road Campus site, which had originally served as a Catholic all-girls high school, was becoming increasingly obsolescent, and so a new thirty-two-acre multi-building site at 8200 West Outer Drive was acquired from the University of Detroit Mercy. While it was necessary to raze several older buildings, others could be retrofitted for use. A campus master plan and massive facility and site-redevelopment effort, augmented in part by state-matching funds in 2009, produced a state-of-the-art Health Sciences Center supporting many career programs, including dental hygiene, emergency medical technology, occupational therapy, phlebotomy, pharmacy technology and healthcare renewable technology.

Chapter 5

BARRIERS TO TRANSPORTATION

At the time the Birwood Wall was constructed, one could walk its length, close up and unimpeded. Today, walking down Birwood Street from Eight Mile Road to Norfolk, the Wall is barely visible, except where Alfonso Wells Playground opens up to expose the colorful murals that stretch for nearly the length of a football field. Otherwise, overgrown bushes, backyard garages and chain link fences obscure a clear view. The Wall, hidden as it is, abruptly stops at the sidewalk on Norfolk to permit entrance and egress, by foot or by automobile, before it continues south again to Chippewa, where it reopens again and then continues to its terminus at Pembroke. One wonders if the real estate developer who built the Wall would have preferred to wall off Norfolk and Chippewa Streets as well. If the Wall were built to make development more secure, then prohibiting entrance and egress would have seemed appropriate. Alter Road on Detroit's East Side is blocked for precisely that reason, to prevent entrance into or egress from Grosse Pointe. As it turns out, the Wall is easy to circumnavigate or, for the more athletic children, climb over to play, as kids do—and did in 1941.

So, if the Wall was not built, in a strict sense, for security, it must have been built for a "sense" of security, as a symbolic reminder of the important differences between "us" and "them." And what must the Wall have communicated to the residents of West Eight Mile Road, particularly after a later developer to the south had attempted to extend the Wall along Pembroke to further isolate the community? Could the Wall have been an attempt to

Children posing in front of Birwood Wall, 1941. *Library of Congress.*

diminish, at least psychologically, the constitutional right to come and go as one pleases, as Justice William Douglas opined in *Kent v. Dulles* (1958): "The right to travel is part of the 'liberty' of which the citizen cannot be deprived without due process of law under the Fifth Amendment....Freedom of movement across frontiers in either direction, and inside frontiers as well, was a part of our heritage....It may be as close to the heart of the individual as the choice of what he eats, or wears, or reads. Freedom of movement is basic in our scheme of values."

However, the *right* to come and go is not synonymous with the *ability* to come and go. For many West Eight Mile Road residents, getting to work, to school, to scheduled medical and dental appointments and even to grocery shopping continues to present major difficulties. The transportation system in metropolitan Detroit is broken, and living right next to a major six-lane thoroughfare like Eight Mile Road offers only the illusion of movement.

During its humble beginnings, even navigating out of the house and getting to Eight Mile could be a chore. As Ruth Rosa Green, another early settler in the area, recalled:

Even in the winter, the shoveling of snow was a team effort, clearing a path from one house to the next and to the main road. I remember our trips to downtown Detroit. It was before buses ran along Eight Mile, so we had to walk or hitch a ride on a farm wagon to Woodward Avenue. There we could take an interurban car, which resembled a combination of a train and streetcar, powered by electricity.[91]

In those days, automobiles that were actually functioning were few and far between.

Marvel Daines's 1941 survey of every tenth family in the community reported the status of car ownership: "Sixteen families out of the 48, or approximately one-third, own cars. However, seven of them won't run—some haven't been out of their muddy rut in the backyard for five years; yet to their owners, the mere fact of their standing there is a matter of pride—they regard the car as an asset."[92] Only five cars are 1936 or later models. While no recent surveys of the West Eight Mile community have been conducted, many residents today suggest car ownership to be less than 50 percent. In this particular ZIP code—and throughout the city of Detroit—the price of owning and operating a motor vehicle is prohibitive.

Without a robust regional transportation system, car ownership would seem to be a necessity, but for Detroiters, the cost to maintain a mechanically sound, properly insured vehicle is dramatically more than in comparable urban areas. Even discounting depreciation, normal maintenance, replacement tires, unexpected repairs and the high cost of fuel, the cost of car insurance in Detroit is staggeringly high. Drivers living in densely populated urban areas like Detroit generally pay more for car insurance than drivers living in suburban and rural areas. However, an August 2014 Quadrant Information Services study, commissioned by InsuranceQuotes.com, examined the cost of insurance premiums in the country's twenty-five largest metropolitan areas and discovered that Detroit drivers pay an astounding 165 percent more than the national average.[93] The report does not account for the causes, but a 2017 *Detroit Free Press* report identified eight major determinants: (1) unique no-fault insurance, which in Michigan pays unlimited medical benefits and accounts for more than 40 percent of a typical policy; (2) motor-vehicle theft, which accounts for more than one-third of all such incidents statewide; (3) carjackings, which, while on the decline, still number several hundred per year; (4) car crashes, which occur in numbers much larger in Detroit than in any state municipality; (5) credit scores, which hurt residents in cities like Detroit with high poverty rates; (6) lack of private health insurance, which results in the use of the medical benefits portion of no-fault policies; and (7) ZIP codes, which auto insurers use to set rates for individuals in areas where the high cost of claims originate.[94]

For Detroiters seeking to obtain or maintain relatively low-wage employment in any of the fifty-odd job-rich municipalities in the northern or western suburbs that have "opted out" of public transit, a car may be the only option. Thousands of Detroiters (and Highland Parkers and Hamtramckers) make the trip every day to these far-flung suburbs like Livonia and Canton Township to the west and Rochester Hills and Orion Township to the north. Part of the problem, officials in these communities claim, is that local residents neither want nor need such a service and have no intention of subsidizing a bus service for those outside their community who do.

EARLY PUBLIC TRANSIT

Detroit's public transit system dates back to 1863, when the city spent $5,000 to buy a fleet of streetcars under the management of the Detroit City Railway Company. By November, three distinct horse-drawn trolley routes—along Woodward, Gratiot and Michigan Avenues—all converged near the Detroit River at Woodward and Jefferson Avenue. From 1892 to 1900, electric streetcars replaced horse-drawn trolleys and service expanded into the suburbs.

From 1901 to 1922, regional transit was operated by a Cleveland syndicate made up of six interurban operations under the name Detroit United Railway (DUR). This period is filled with opportunity to create and implement a truly city-suburban regional transportation system. In 1919, such a plan was developed by the Detroit Rapid Transit Commission, which recommended a multi-modal system. However, in 1920, Mayor James Couzens believed that streetcars were the backbone of any Detroit-area transportation system and vetoed a bond issue to build a subway system. The city council attempted to override the veto but failed by a single vote.

The period from 1922 to 1974 marked a dramatic turn in the history of Detroit regional transit and set the stage for today's bifurcated and disjointed regional transportation system. In 1922, following a voter-approved plan to build and operate a municipally owned transit operation, Detroit purchased the DUR for just under $20 million and renamed the

Mayor James Couzens at wheel of new bus, undated. *Walter P. Reuther Library, Archives of Labor and Urban Affairs, Wayne State University.*

system the Department of Street Railways (DSR), with 1,457 streetcars operated by more than four thousand city employees.

One of the remarkable aspects of this period in Detroit's transportation history is the level of African American participation in its day-to-day operations. Prior to 1922, few blacks found employment anywhere within Detroit's transportation system, except "for laying tracks and in various menial jobs."[95] Following the election of James Couzens as mayor, however, the black community found a sympathetic ear at city hall, and through the offices of the Detroit Urban League, significant strides were made in African American recruitment and hiring. For the first time, blacks were driving and maintaining buses and trolleys, though not without significant backlash from white passengers, who complained about good civil service jobs being taken from them. By 1942, the dramatic influx of southern blacks and whites was putting tremendous strain on the public transportation system. City residents without cars or the fuel to operate them due to war rationing were dependent on the DSR to take them to various employment centers scattered across the nearly forty square miles of the city. The number of passengers on the combined bus and trolley lines increased from 30,811,660 in 1940 to 34,171,174 in 1941 to

45,033,989 in 1942.[96] Racial confrontation gradually escalated from verbal to physical on the overcrowded and fully integrated bus service, exacerbated by deeply ingrained prejudices of transplanted southerners. The battle lines for social equality were being drawn during the war in the city's public transportation system.

In 1931, a railway commuter service between Detroit and Pontiac was offered by the Grand Trunk Western Railroad. Soon another such rail line service was established between Detroit and Ann Arbor. Riders of the system now had the choice of between buses, streetcars and commuter rail services. Detroit voters even approved a subway plan, but the state advisory board refused to recommend construction to the federal government. Meanwhile, DSR general manager Fred Nolan began his push to replace streetcars with buses but did not see his campaign achieve fruition until 1956, when streetcar service ended after nearly a century of continuous operation. The 1940s generally represent the high point for the metropolitan Detroit regional transit system, serving 490 million riders annually. By the mid-1950s, with the infusion of federal highway dollars for the construction of new roads and expressways, the writing was on the wall: a balanced system of highways and mass transit was the new regional imperative, and the city of Detroit now began its gradual depopulation.

A WINDOW OF OPPORTUNITY SLOWLY CLOSES

Historically, the most promising opportunity to develop and implement a comprehensive regional transportation system for southeast Michigan came during the sixteen-year period of 1964 to 1980. As part of Lyndon Johnson's "Great Society" urban initiatives, the federal government began to provide funding to subsidize urban projects, including mass transit. Despite conservative resistance to federal involvement in efforts to resolve urban problems, the urban Mass Transportation Act was passed by Congress and signed into law in 1964. The act specifically authorized the secretary of transportation to assist in the development of comprehensive and coordinated mass transportation systems for such major economic centers as Detroit, Philadelphia and Los Angeles. The Department of Transportation offered to fund two-thirds of urban mass transit projects and to that end provided $375 million for a preliminary three-year period to fund transit studies and demonstration projects. Following the 1967 Detroit civil disorder, the Metropolitan Fund and the new Detroit Committee, a unique coalition of business, labor and government leaders, came together in support of legislation creating the Southeast Michigan Council of Governments (SEMCOG) and the Southeast Michigan Transportation Authority (SEMTA) to coordinate and qualify the region for the federal funding.

Even as a moderate Republican, Governor William Milliken struck a tone of progressive reform in matters of comprehensive regional transportation. His commitment to Michigan cities was reflected in his creation of a state Urban Affairs office located strategically in Detroit, to further coordinate efforts to address urban issues, including mass transit, and particularly to provide a conduit with which to foster cooperation between state and local government. Unfortunately, elements within the state legislature were constructing roadblocks to disrupt if not disband the two regional bodies, SEMCOG and SEMTA, created to develop and implement mass transit throughout metropolitan Detroit. Various bills threatened the funding and organization of SEMCOG specifically or imposed such restrictive procedures so as to interfere with its basic functions.

Despite substantial suburban and outstate legislative resistance, SEMCOG and SEMTA were making slow but steady progress in developing a series of transportation improvement projects designed to demonstrate regional cooperation to the federal government, which would be funding these and more sophisticated projects. Even as these smaller projects were being developed and funded, SEMTA was looking at the big picture. Using Detroit's Central Business District (CBD) as the axis of all things mass transit, SEMTA developed by 1971 a comprehensive plan for the region, the first phase of which would include an underground rail line to transport commuters from the CBD up Woodward Avenue to Eight Mile Road and the fairgrounds, the baseline separating Detroit and Wayne County from Oakland County, a major suburban population center. The subway system would, in the future, extend into Oakland County to Eleven Mile Road, whereupon the rail line would resurface and continue on along the Grand Trunk Western right-of-way embankment and terminate as an elevated line in Pontiac.

Deep structural barriers in the 1970s dashed any hope of creating a mass transit system for metropolitan Detroit. Although Michigan native son President Gerald R. Ford committed $600 million in federal funding to build such a system, three factors mitigated against its construction: fragmented suburban interests and increasing outstate resistance brought on by legislative reapportionment that gave greater voice to outstate and rural interests, the inability of SEMCOG and SEMTA to levy taxes to support their agenda and the sometimes locally ambivalent voice of a city built on the back of the automotive industry. With the inauguration of conservative Republican Ronald Reagan in 1980, federal funding for such regional projects evaporated and ended any rational hope that such barriers might eventually be overcome.

In 1985, Amtrak proposed building a passenger rail station at the Joe Louis Arena to restart commuter service between Detroit and Ann Arbor, which had been terminated the year before by the fledgling Southeast Michigan Transportation Authority (SEMTA). The project was dropped, however, when its offer to match funds with local developers failed. A few years later, the People Mover was built downtown at a cost of $67 million per mile. The DSR was now reorganized as the Detroit Department of Transportation (DDOT). In 1989, SEMTA, which had originally been formed to reorganize the bus services throughout Wayne, Oakland and Macomb Counties, as well as the city of Detroit, reorganized once again—this time excluding the city of Detroit—and rebranded itself the Suburban Mobility Authority for Regional Transportation (SMART). Repeated attempts by DDOT and SMART officials to merge major bus routes and establish a common regional bus pass failed.

In 2009, Governor Jennifer Granholm signed legislation enabling the formation of private, nonprofit entities to build a light rail service. Immediately, the M1Rail was launched as the first such private entity to build a light rail line, dubbed the QLINE after Quicken Loans, which bought the naming rights, from Congress Street downtown to its northern terminus at Grand Boulevard in the New Center area. The QLINE greeted its first riders in May 2017, and daily ridership hovers around three thousand, although the number is difficult to estimate any more precisely because no more than 40 percent actually pay the requested fare. Finally, in 2016, a failed millage proposal to finally establish a true regional transportation system failed in the tri-county area by 18,000 out of more than 1.8 million votes cast. The new system, funded for twenty years with a 1.2 mill property tax assessment, would have placed rapid transit bus lines on major regional transit corridors and added commuter rail between Detroit and Ann Arbor. Officials from the "Big Four"—Wayne, Oakland and Macomb Counties and the city of Detroit—met regularly but failed in an attempt to place a new proposal on the ballot in 2018.

THE HISTORY OF PUBLIC TRANSIT ALONG WEST EIGHT MILE ROAD

As part of Detroit's transit history, Eight Mile Road did not begin to see regular bus service until the city bought the DUR and began managing its own transit system. In November 1924, the new DSR established a bus route along Eight Mile Road, but since it did not own or operate any of its own buses, it contracted out the service to the Detroit Motorbus Company. Once the city received delivery of an adequate fleet of its own buses, the DSR took over the route in the middle of the year 1925.[97]

The impetus for launching the service along Eight Mile Road was to service prospective local employees of Henry Ford's Highland Park (Model T) Assembly Plant, where workers could earn the staggering sum of five dollars for a day's work. As West Eight Mile's population grew as a result of the worker influx during the First World War, bus service would transport workers directly to and from the Ford factory at Woodward and Manchester. The return trip took workers back as far as Eight Mile and Turner, just west of Livernois. Months later, the route was revised whereby workers could board the bus as far west as Wyoming, depart the bus at the fairgrounds and then board the Woodward bus south to Highland Park. The Woodward streetcar line had just recently been extended to the fairgrounds, making the transit connection for Ford workers living in the West Eight Mile community convenient and efficient.

During the Second World War, the West Eight Mile Road bus route was renamed Eight Mile West, and upon its arriving at its terminus, the fairgrounds, passengers would board an electrified Woodward Avenue streetcar traveling south to Highland Park instead of the customary diesel-powered bus. As part of the war effort to conserve rubber and fuel, the Department of Defense banned all bus lines that duplicated streetcar routes. June 14, 1944, marked the date when the Eight Mile West bus route was completely revamped. Instead of the fairgrounds at Woodward being the terminus of the Eight Mile route, the bus continued along Eight Mile to Conant Avenue on Detroit's east side. In 1956, the bus route was extended west along Eight Mile Road to Inkster Road, picking up shoppers from Northland Shopping Center. For the next fifty years, the Eight Mile bus route would experience interruptions, discontinuations, schedule changes and route adjustments as the entire system underwent reorganization of services following financial difficulties within the DSR and a thorough needs assessment by the new DDOT.

New bus trolley, December 14, 1949. *Walter P. Reuther Library, Archives of Labor and Urban Affairs, Wayne State University.*

Today, DDOT operates the Eight Mile bus line, identified simply as Route 17. The route starts at Seven Mile Road and Five Points Street at the border of Detroit and Redford Township, proceeds east to Lahser Road and travels north on Lahser to Eight Mile, whereupon the bus turns east on Eight Mile, crosses Woodward Avenue and proceeds along southbound Kelly Road on the far east side; then it turns back east on Moross and completes its journey at Mack Avenue and Moross in Harper Woods. For workers living in the West Eight Mile community, Route 17 makes stops every day at the Belmont Shopping Center, Chrysler Warren Truck Assembly plant, the Eight Mile/Dequindre Commercial District, the Eight Mile/Gratiot Commercial District and the Seven Mile/Telegraph Commercial District.

For carless West Eight Mile residents working or traveling directly south, Route 54 starts at Eight Mile Road and proceeds south along Wyoming Avenue all the way to Dearborn. The route stops at various employment centers, including the Chrysler McGraw Glass Plant, Truck City, Ford River Rouge Plant, Kingswood Hospital, Royal Town Center, State Fair Transit Center and the Wyoming/Curtis Commercial District.

With the job sprawl in metropolitan Detroit among the worst in the nation for urban residents to connect to outlying jobs-rich suburban communities like Livonia and Canton Township, Detroit workers may have to opt for ride-sharing services like Uber or Lyft to complete the journey from the closest bus drop-off point. For short local trips, such as grocery shopping or a dentist appointment, ride-sharing services such as GM's Maven or ZipCar are available to West Eight Mile residents. Though originally aimed at a younger millennial-based demographic, Maven is a car-sharing service where cars are rented through a smartphone app and typically used for short trips. One of the advantages of Maven is that a range of vehicles is available from Chevy Cruze and Volt (at eight dollars per hour) to an SUV for family use, such as Chevy Tahoe or Cadillac Escalade. Presently Maven has five locations in Detroit.

SPECIAL TRANSIT PROGRAMS

In August 2018, city school officials unveiled a new transportation system for K–8 students in the Northwest Detroit community. The program, GOAL (Get On and Learn) Line, is designed to provide a safe, efficient and closely monitored bus service from the school location nearest to one's home to the destination school. Currently, four charter schools and six Detroit public schools participate. After students are dismissed from their primary school of choice at the end of the day, they are picked up by the bus service and transported to the Northwest Activities Center on Meyers Road for an after-school program and then returned to the school closest to their home in the evening. Participating children receive a swipe card to use at pickup and drop-off points, allowing parents to keep tabs on their children via a text message. Detroit Public Schools participating include Bagley Elementary, Coleman A. Young Elementary, the Foreign Language Immersion and Cultural Studies School, John R. King Academic & Performing Arts Academy, the Schulze Academy for Technology and Arts and—for most of the West Eight Mile community students—Vernor Elementary. The charter schools include Cornerstone Lincoln-King Academy, Detroit Achievement Academy, McDowell Preparatory Academy and the university YES Academy. At the Northwest Activities Center, students can opt to participate in a range of enrichment activities, including robotics, arts and crafts and academic tutoring, as well as physical education programs in swimming and

Eastern Market signage. *Author's collection.*

basketball. Trained teachers, counselors and security officers are on-site and engaged during all activities.

A strategic objective of the GOAL Line is to boost enrollment in both Detroit public schools and at charter schools by making its bus service and after-school programs attractive to parents. Currently, as many as thirty-two thousand Detroit parents send their children to suburban school districts, leaving many of Detroit's two hundred schools underutilized. An additional impetus to keep children is the fact that some of the schools in the GOAL Line loop report higher test scores than some of the schools for which students are leaving Detroit.

Another special program undertaken for the benefit of Northwest Detroit residents is the product of a partnership between DDOT, Eastern Market and the Department of Health. The program was created to address the issue of food insufficiency by providing fresh, locally processed meats, dairy products and farm produce. Called Fresh Wagon, the program offers Northwest Detroit residents a round-trip Saturday morning bus trip to Detroit's famed Eastern Market, which boasts more than two hundred food and horticultural product vendors. The new program allows riders an hour and a half to shop at the various open-air farm market stalls, as well as the numerous nearby stores along Russell Street, not to mention Gratiot Central

Market on nearby Gratiot Avenue. The ride to the Eastern Market costs $1.50 each way, but seniors pay only $1 for the round-trip. The point of origin for the bus trip is Seven Mile and Evergreen Roads. Eastern Market is an ideal venue for Northwest Detroiters on a fixed income who would benefit from access to wholesome, reasonably priced meats, dairy and produce.

Chapter 6

BARRIERS TO HEALTHCARE

T he context of one's life determines one's health, and a basic understanding of such factors as inheritance, access to clinical treatment and one's social and physical environment can lead to corrective action. For generations of African Americans in Detroit, significant societal barriers, memorialized by the Birwood Wall, have made quality healthcare extremely difficult or even unattainable.

Establishing a hospital to serve the needs of the West Eight Mile community was a major goal of Franciscan Father Alvin Deem following the dedication of Our Lady of Victory.[98] Intuitively, Father Deem knew that tending to the physical needs of his congregation was inseparable from tending to their spiritual needs. The fact that he was transferred out of the area by the archdiocese before he could achieve his goal was a missed opportunity. The Detroit Urban League, too, was well aware that community healthcare needed to be addressed, even though its new community center on Northlawn could only accommodate a small clinic, staffed part time by a local doctor and a nurse.[99] The bigger issue was how and where does one obtain comprehensive healthcare and clinical treatment as medical issues arise?

An opportunity to address the issue was missed when, in 1940, Marvel Daines surveyed residents of the Eight Mile community and failed to incorporate into her study any information pertaining to the physical well-being of the community. She had skirted the issue with inquiries about school attendance and frequent colds from drafty bedrooms and had fielded random complaints about food insufficiency. However, connecting the dots between the determinants of health that she did study—housing, employment, transportation and education—and the ultimate well-being of the community's residents either never occurred to her or was seen as beyond the scope of the inquiry.

THE STATE OF AFRICAN AMERICAN HEALTHCARE

In many respects, the physical health and well-being of the residents of West Eight Mile Road can be treated in a manner similar to that of other working-class blacks in Detroit. There were no hospitals or specialty clinics catering to the special needs of the community beyond the aforementioned DUL clinic. The same hospitals and clinics that served the larger African American population south of Eight Mile were available to the Eight Mile community—save the greater distance in traveling to access them.

Regardless of where in Detroit one received medical treatment, racial discrimination and segregation of services helped to explain why African Americans suffered the worst healthcare treatment, the worst health status and the worst health outcomes of any race or ethnic group being treated. Racial discrimination in one form or another permeated every aspect of healthcare, from discriminatory hiring practices with respect to doctors, nurses, orderlies and other clinical staffing to inferior treatment for various conditions or even withholding treatment for those conditions. Racial discrimination even affected the insurance billing industry, which routinely accepted, rejected or adjusted claims based on the race of the claimant and paid different rates to the provider of services based on the same.[100]

The enormous gap between the health of Detroit's white and black residents in 1940 is reflected in the overall mortality rates (8.0 versus 11.3 per thousand), infant mortality rates (2.9 versus 3.6 per thousand) and maternal mortality (36.0 versus 50.8 per thousand). Except for accidents and cancer, African Americans registered significantly higher rates in such categories as heart disease, pneumonia and venereal disease. When one factors in that whites possessed more vehicles and lived, on average, ten years longer than their black counterpart, the higher accident and cancer diagnoses are understandable. Especially troubling, however, was that the death rate due to tuberculosis (168 per hundred thousand) was seven times that of whites statewide.[101]

A decade later, the statistical correlation between race and selective diseases remained. In 1951, the Detroit Urban League studied particular wholly manageable diseases such as pneumonia and tuberculosis that afflicted blacks disproportionately due to discriminatory hospital and clinical practices in Detroit. To dramatize the "brutal callousness" to which African Americans were subjected, the DUL cited the following case study as representative:

> *On October 8, 1951, at 7:30 p.m., Mrs. Roosevelt Walton, a Negro mother, brought her baby to Dr. Thornton's office in Ecorse. The doctor gave the child immediate attention because it was evident the child was seriously ill. He diagnosed the case as bronchial pneumonia and urged the mother to take her baby to* CHILDREN'S HOSPITAL *immediately as the child needed oxygen.*
>
> *Mrs. Walton arrived at* CHILDREN'S HOSPITAL *at 8:05 p.m. and gave the receptionist a letter she had gotten from Dr. Thornton indicating the nature of the case. Mrs. Walton was told to wait her turn. After waiting over an hour, she again approached the receptionist but was told again to wait. Mrs. Walton became hysterical as she saw the condition of her baby became worse. A gentleman in the waiting room came over to look at the baby. He screamed, "This baby is dying." The nurses ran to the baby and took the child to the examining room. But it was too late. The baby had died.*[102]

The origins of the African American healthcare crisis can be traced back to the population explosion in the run-up to World War I and the segregationist mentality of whites supervising medical education and clinical training and administering the city's hospitals and clinics. Obtaining a medical education as a black undergraduate was fraught with barriers designed to discourage even the bravest souls. Admission locally to Wayne State University's medical School was normally selective, but for African Americans it was nearly impossible. At that time, Wayne would take one black entrant and maybe two Jewish entrants per year. Most did not bother to apply. For the few who did, even an extraordinary record of undergraduate accomplishment might be insufficient for serious consideration. Instead, most had to leave the state to attend institutions where their applications would be taken more seriously, such as at historically black schools like Meharry Medical College or Howard University College of Medicine. Afterward, obtaining a hospital internship or medical residency became another gauntlet. In order for a black physician in Detroit to become a surgeon, he or she became a resident at one of the black hospitals, where, in many instances, a large patient load of severely ill people were waiting. Municipal hospitals, which operated on a black patient quota system, would often admit blacks whose situations promised to be useful teaching cases and transfer the remaining to the small black hospitals—if they had space to take them.

With rare exception, black physicians who applied for staff positions and admitting privileges to both municipal and by proprietary hospitals were rejected. Furthermore, proprietary hospitals rejected black patients wholesale; municipal hospitals operated on a quota system. If one had seriously ill patients, one had to persuade a white colleague to admit them to the hospital. Such a policy had serious consequences. As Lionel Swan, MD, recalled:

> I had called a white colleague who agreed to hospitalize a woman who I diagnosed as possible kidney failure. When she reached the hospital and her husband, not knowing the name of the white doctor, stated her doctor was Dr. Swan, the admitting clerk recognizing the name as that of a black doctor obviously not on the hospital staff, refused to admit the patient. She died shortly thereafter on the same day. There was a universal outcry of condemnation of the clerk's action, but nothing was done except possibly a promise to use better discretion in the future.[103]

To provide better training for black physicians and more comprehensive care for black patients, a handful of physicians opened private black-owned hospitals. The first was Dunbar Hospital, named after the famous black poet Paul Lawrence Dunbar. Thirty black physicians, led by Dr. James W. Ames, purchased the old Charles W. Warren house just west of Woodward Avenue on Frederick Street and formed the Allied Medical Society to promote the health and well-being of the African American community. In the years following, more than a dozen black proprietary hospitals opened in Detroit, including Kirkwood, Edyth K. Thomas, Trinity, Burton Mercy and, most recently, Southwest Detroit General Hospital in 1974, which was a consolidation of four smaller proprietary hospitals in southwest Detroit—Boulevard General, Burton Mercy, Delray General and Trumbull General. These hospitals were small, often former family homes retrofitted to accommodate as many patient beds as possible. Sometimes a four-family flat was reorganized to serve fifteen or twenty patients.

Compared to the large municipal hospitals, the small black proprietary hospitals must have seemed primitive. Detroit physician Dr. Waldo Cain,

Dunbar Hospital at 580 Frederick Street, Detroit. *Author's collection.*

a graduate of all-black Meharry Medical School in Nashville, recalled the conditions under which doctors at such facilities had to work:

> *I can recall seeing a patient with intestinal obstruction at old Kirkwood Hospital, and we didn't have a suction machine. Even at Meharry we could hook them up to wall suction. They had these little portable suctions at Kirkwood, but the thing didn't work. It's 3 a.m., and I have this tube down this patient, and the wall suction won't work. They only had one. What I had to do was tell a nursing supervisor to give me an aide and let the aide sit there with a big syringe and just syringe all night long. But it worked. It was the most primitive kind of thing, but they worked. People got well. It took a lot of imagination on the part of the surgeon.*[104]

After World War II, the proprietary hospitals began to disappear. Unable to compete with the larger, well-equipped, technology-enhanced public institutions, hospitals like Kirkwood faced increasing scrutiny from accrediting agencies. In the 1960s, federal funding from Medicare and Medicaid imposed stringent standards these institutions could not meet. Southwest Detroit Hospital, the last of such institutions in Detroit, which had cost $21 million to accommodate 246 patient beds, survived for just sixteen years.

Adding to the inadequacy of resources to meet the needs of African Americans, there were too few black physicians to treat too many patients. Many black citizens were already fearful of hospitals based on a long-standing belief that hospital doctors used laboratory tests to conduct experiments on patients. In this era before the development of sulfa drugs, there was also the legitimate and well-documented fear of contracting a serious infection while under a doctor's care in a hospital. As a result, many African Americans in Detroit sought alternative forms of treatment outside the conventional medical establishment.

Alternative health practitioners serving the black community fell into two categories: spiritualists and independent specialists. Spiritualists, or "Divine Healers," as some preferred to be called, typically offered variations of the tent revival's "laying of the hands." Forrester Washington, the first director of the Detroit Urban League, remembered dealing with a particular spiritualist: "One of these healers started in business only a month ago charging 50 cents a treatment. He has built up such a following that he is now charging from $2.00 to $25.00, according to the amount he thinks a patient will be able to pay. His office is always full of sick blacks who get up early in the morning to be first in line when his place of business opens."[105]

A second category of alternative medicine practitioner was the independent specialist. These herbalists, neighborhood prophets and magic store vendors treated a broad range of physical and mental ailments. Such treatments might have included mystical or religious rituals, the use of roots and herbs and specific directives on what to do or avoid once the patient was home. Not only had the Great Migration brought tens of thousands of blacks from the rural South to work in Detroit's factories, but the Diaspora also brought with it a wealth of African folklore, Christian and Vodoun religion, as well as family traditions passed down from one generation to the next, all of which many blacks in Detroit were predisposed to utilize as an antidote to the discriminatory practices they experienced.

Troubled by the poor health of Detroit's black population, the Detroit Urban League launched an observance of National Negro Health Week. Booker T. Washington, founder of the Tuskegee Institute, issued a call for blacks across the nation to join with him in a movement designed to aid in improving health conditions, which he saw as impediments to economic success and, thereby, acceptance into the mainstream of American society. Economic success was seen by Washington as rooted in the pursuits of education, business, property ownership and racial unity.

In 1915, Washington launched the first Health Improvement Week with the cooperation of local organizations and agencies across the country that were in a position to reach and influence the greatest number of African Americans.

In Detroit, under the direction and supervision of John Dancy, the DUL enlisted the aid of physicians to talk to various African American congregations throughout the city on a range of practical health-related topics such as personal hygiene or proper sanitation techniques. In 1919, the DUL established a baby clinic on Columbia Street, staffed by a doctor and three nurses. Five mornings a week, black mothers brought their babies to the clinic, sometimes as many as fifty a day, to be examined and receive clinical instruction on the baby's care and feeding. Many of the mothers had come to Detroit from the rural South and were completely unfamiliar with the state of medical science and had never been attended to by a physician. For many, Dancy concluded, it was eye opening:

> *Their views, based on their childhood training, clashed with those of the medical profession. Some had been taught that the way to ward off sickness for their children was to hang a bag of asafetida around the child's neck. Another, more modern school of thought held that the best thing to hang around the neck was a dime. It was quite disconcerting to some of the mothers to find that the doctors held even more radical views. "Take the dime off the baby's neck and buy him some milk with it," one doctor said. "It will do him more good."*[106]

The baby clinic was such a success that it continued for many years thereafter. The National Negro Health Week lasted until 1951, at which point the U.S. Department of Public Health attempted to integrate community services on the federal level.

HEALTH CRISIS IN ROYAL OAK TOWNSHIP

Between 1940 and 1950, the population of Royal Oak Township increased from 1,724 to 10,448. This sixfold increase was the direct result of the federal government funneling large numbers of African American war workers into the segregated, hastily constructed war housing units built along the West Eight Mile corridor. By 1950, 74 percent, or 1,709 of 2,300 dwelling units in the township, were seriously dilapidated, requiring clearance or major rehabilitation. At the same time, nearly half of the housing units were overcrowded—the worst overcrowding in the metropolitan area.

A polio epidemic—although some official controversy existed as to whether this was an actual epidemic—hit the metropolitan Detroit area in 1958. There were more reported cases in Royal Oak Township than the surrounding suburban communities. Most of the communities had already started polio clinics. Eventually, 2,500 shots were administered at the Carver School. Although shots were available for Grant School, people affiliated with the Ferndale School District enabled them to obtain shots in Ferndale.

The major health problems as reported by the Oakland County Board of Health included very high rates of tuberculosis, venereal disease, infant mortality, illegitimacy and lack of knowledge of proper dietary standards. The township recorded the highest infant mortality rate in the state at 11 percent, far above the public health rate.[107] Lack of education about and access to local healthcare complicated an already dire situation. The County Health Department provided free clinic facilities for venereal disease control, a dental clinic for children, immunization clinic for children under fourteen and referral services for other problems. But the clinic was some six miles away, expensive and time-consuming to reach by public transportation, and hence it was not utilized as much as it should have been. Medical care on a free or very low-cost basis for indigent or low-income families was available only in Pontiac, some eighteen miles away, or in Detroit; the distances, cost of getting to clinics and hospitals and the time involved made the use of such facilities very difficult.

The hospitals open to township residents in Pontiac were St. Joseph's and Pontiac General. In Detroit, township residents could receive service from Harper Hospital, Henry Ford, Parkside, Women's, Mount Carmel Mercy and Sinai Hospitals, both clinics and in-patient. In addition, North End Clinic also served township residents. The closest of these facilities was about ten miles, while in terms of time by public transportation, the closest clinic or hospital in Detroit was nearly a half hour away and the furthest more than one hour. By car, Detroit facilities could be reached in from ten to thirty-five minutes.

THE SOCIAL AND ECONOMIC DETERMINANTS OF HEALTH: A SUMMARY

Society wields considerable influence over the health and well-being of its citizens. Government entities enact laws and regulatory measures, allocate resources and take actions designed, in theory, to advance the public good. Public policy has had a striking impact in such areas as housing, employment, education and transportation. These four areas of influence—referred to by experts as the social and economic determinants of health—have historically bestowed certain advantages on particular groups while erecting barriers for others. The Birwood Wall memorializes these barriers, particularly as they have affected African Americans in metropolitan Detroit.

Following the Great Depression, the federal government enacted legislation and created "New Deal" agencies designed to kick-start the economy. In his first one hundred days in office, Franklin Delano Roosevelt pushed Congress to pass sixteen new laws and agencies, including the Emergency Farm Mortgage Act, which provided loans to save farms from foreclosure; the Home Owners Refinancing Act, which established the Home Owners Loan Corporation (HOLC), which refinanced mortgages to prevent foreclosure (by 1935, it had refinanced 1 million homes, or 20 percent of all urban mortgages); and the National Housing Act, which established the Federal Housing Administration (FHA), which provided federal insurance on mortgages.

HOLC's residential security maps, color-coded to distinguish levels of desirability for real estate investment, had the effect of promoting the growth of racially homogenous, single-family suburban housing developments to the detriment of urban and black and integrated neighborhoods. With maps in hand, private sector banks and mortgage brokers could claim justification for wholesale rejection of loan applications from African Americans. The ingenious plan of a real estate developer in northwest Detroit to construct a concrete wall between the existing redlined black enclave of West Eight Mile Road and his new development to the west underscored the segregationist mentality that would take years to overcome.

Another effect of redlining was the perpetuation of substandard housing, which further contributed to the disparities in health between low- and higher-income homeowners. Substandard housing—the kind described by Marvel Daines in her report on the West Eight Mile enclave—was not simply old or outdated but posed distinct health risks

Children playing at the side of a house on Birwood Street, 1941. The Wall is in the background. *Library of Congress.*

from structural issues, poor ventilation, unsafe electrical service, leaking roofs, non-insulated walls, poorly maintained heating systems and the lack of clean drinking water.

Working conditions are a significant determiner of health as well. Before World War II, black migrants from the South usually had to settle for jobs in the service sector, such as janitorial work, or in menial farm labor rather than in the better-paying automobile factories. If one was particularly lucky or had made the right connection, a job might be offered in one of the few auto companies hiring blacks, such as Ford, Briggs or Dodge. The job situation would improve greatly during the Second World War, when line workers of all stripes were needed for war production in the newly converted auto manufacturing plants. The jobs were largely unskilled positions, often the dirtiest and most dangerous jobs in the least desirable departments in the factory. Even after the war, when automation and decentralization eliminated many of the unskilled positions formerly held by blacks in the remaining Detroit-area factories, continued racial discrimination made working in the factories a living nightmare.

Within the factory environment, blacks faced racial abuse, shop floor violence and horrendous working conditions resulting in long-term health issues. Racial abuse took many forms, from foremen and coworkers hurtling insults and racial epithets to speed-up demands and accusations of laziness cast in particularly offensive stereotypical language. Shop floor violence before, during and after shift change was not uncommon, particularly in the rare instance when a black was promoted to a position whites felt they were passed over for.

Health issues surfaced most dramatically in the actual working conditions on the shop floor. Blacks were subjected to the dirtiest, most labor-intensive and most hazardous areas of the plant. Each area or department, however, had its particular set of health issues. In the River Rouge Plant's massive blast furnaces and foundries, or in the toxic air environment of the paint shops, blacks were most often found.

The workplace environment for African Americans contributed to a disproportionate degree of exposure to dangerous toxic elements. In the paint shops, for example, black workers were exposed to solvents, additives and other chemicals used in the vehicle painting process, leading to increased risk of several kinds of occupation-related cancers such as lung, bladder and pancreatic cancer. In the blast furnaces and foundries, workers were exposed to molten metal explosions, heat exhaustion and stroke, severe burns and eye disorders from ultraviolet or infrared radiation emanating from the molten metal.

Other areas of the factory offered constant exposure to asbestos, as the heating pipes and water pipes were wrapped in a fabric containing the deadly silicate mineral. Asbestos was also used in the manufacture of brake shoes and clutch plates. Lung scarring and many different cancers—including lung, colon, esophagus and stomach cancer—were the outcomes of such exposure, although symptoms might not develop for years. A union benefit representative once claimed, with unmistakable gallows humor, that he could determine what department employees worked from reading the death certificates.

A third determinant of health is one's educational attainment, a strong predictor of long-term health and quality of life. Research studies suggest that educational attainment correlates with self-rated health conditions, infant mortality and life expectancy. Adults with lower levels of educational completion tend to report lower health outcomes; babies of mothers who do not complete high school are twice as likely to die before their first birthday; and college graduates live typically five years longer than those who do not complete high school.

While the social and economic benefits associated with educational attainment are well documented, the drawbacks of racial segregation were articulated by the U.S. Supreme Court in its landmark 1954 ruling in *Brown v. Board of Education*. The Warren Court overturned the Melville Fuller court's ruling in *Plessy v. Ferguson*, which held that as long as separate facilities were equal, segregated schools did not violate the equal protection clause of the Fourteenth Amendment. The Warren Court, on the other hand, held that "separate educational facilities are inherently unequal" and cited contemporary social science research suggesting that segregation had a deleterious effect on black school children's mental status. Moreover, racial segregation as it applied to public education perpetuated inferior teaching, overlooked dated teaching materials, permitted overcrowding and tolerated poor student performance.

Brown intended to directly address racial segregation in the seventeen southern states that required it by law. In the North, however, many city schools operated under de facto segregation, with school boards denying any deliberate or conscious intent to segregate students. However, *Plessy* argued that even de jure segregation was required by the Fourteenth Amendment to provide equal accommodations for all students. In the case of West Eight Mile public schools, particularly Higginbotham in Detroit and Carver and Grant in Royal Oak Township, accommodations were anything but equal. With all three schools, overcrowding was tolerated even as nearby white schools reported available capacity. Furthermore, when Higginbotham was directed to accept additional black students, the older Birdhurst School, in serious disrepair, was reopened to handle the overflow.

A salutary benefit of segregation, if such can even be said, is that it galvanized communities of parents to get involved in local school board issues and elections and helped to energize civil rights activism nationally.

Transportation, too, is a vitally important health determinant particularly for those without access to an automobile. For many residents of working-class neighborhoods, automobile transportation is not a given. Getting to work, to doctors' appointments, to the hospital and to sources of nutritious foods can pose regular problems that result in stress, missed medical treatment, lost wages and overdependence on convenient but unhealthy fast foods. In the 1940s, public transportation was limited, cumbersome and unpredictable. In an emergency medical situation for a resident of Royal Oak Township, the issue was obtaining transport to Pontiac General Hospital or facilities even farther away and more difficult to access. For a resident of the Detroit side of Eight Mile Road, the choice was Receiving

Hospital downtown or a black proprietary hospital downtown, assuming it had capacity and the appropriate facility for the specialty involved.

Given the distance to many suburban centers of employment, consistent, reliable means of transportation—bus, taxi or ride-sharing services such as Uber or Lyft—often involves considerable time and expense, and its complexity threatens job security for urban working-class adults.

Regular and reliable access to healthy, affordable food sources is also a transportation issue. Food insecure children and adults risk obesity, malnutrition and other chronic food-related disorders when the only convenient local option is fast food or the limited options within neighborhood markets.

Genetic predisposition is only one factor in assessing the health of an individual. Access to quality healthcare has been a perennial issue for working-class African Americans in metropolitan Detroit. This issue has been compounded by the living conditions of blacks in the West Eight Mile enclave whose original intentions, ironically, were to take residence in a healthier non-urban environment. Research is finally beginning to establish links between one's general health and such social and economic determinants as housing, employment, education, transportation and other factors.

Chapter 7

BARRIERS TO PUBLIC ACCOMMODATIONS

I was born at my mother's house on Northlawn in Detroit on April 21, 1928. However, we moved to Parkside Street on the north side of Eight Mile when I was very young. My mother had by this time divorced my father and was doing day work until the war. Sometime in the early 1940s, people came door to door seeking workers for the war production factories downtown. My mom and two neighbor ladies were instantly recruited. I remember one lady went to work for Chrysler, another for Briggs and my mother for Turnstead, a small factory at Livernois and Jefferson Avenue.

I had just finished at Taft Junior High and was headed to Lincoln High in Ferndale. Friends of mine from Carver Elementary were being bused to Northern High School in Detroit because Lincoln High School would not accept them. If you went to school east of Wyoming, like I did, you were assigned to Lincoln.

The discrimination I experienced at Lincoln because of my color was mixed. When I tried to enroll in college prep classes, the counselor said, "Wouldn't you like to enroll in the general curriculum? In business classes?" The same was true if you tried to enroll in foreign languages. One girl I know really complained and was finally allowed to take a Spanish class.

Only white children could use the swimming pool. If we complained, we were ignored. You learned after a while to stop complaining. It was just the way it was. After school, a lot of the white kids would meet friends across the street at an ice cream store. We colored kids were not allowed in. We could sit at the counter at the dime store, though.

One time our public speaking teacher, Mr. Walters, sent us downtown to the Cass Theater to see Life with Father, *starring William Powell and Elizabeth Taylor. I was the only black child in the class going. Hiram Williams refused to go because he already*

Marion Baxter. *Author's collection.*

knew how he would be treated downtown. We got in the theater, and an usher saw me and said, "Negroes are not allowed in here!" My classmates made a commotion and I was finally allowed to stay. I was really upset and really did not enjoy the movie after that. I soon learned which movie houses accepted you and which ones simply preferred you go elsewhere. You could go to the Roxy, the Colonial, the Adams and the Broadway Capital. You always wanted to be nicely dressed though. If you went to the Fox, United Artists, the Palms or the Michigan, you were ushered up to the balcony. Sometimes you were able to sneak down to the main floor if you didn't get caught.

Later on that day that I saw Life with Father, *we walked over to Washington Boulevard to get something to eat. I was stopped at the door. This time, nothing my classmates said made a difference. I just told them, "Don't worry about me. Go ahead and have a good time." I caught a bus by myself and headed home.*[108]

Marion Baxter, ninety, currently resides in Royal Oak Township.

A few years after he resigned his position as vice-president and general manager of Ford Motor Company, James Couzens considered running for mayor of Detroit. A close associate suggested to him that he consult with John Dancy of the Detroit Urban League for advice on cultivating the black vote. Couzens subsequently planned a dinner party to engage a group of potential supporters and potential donors, including Dancy and a handful of the other influential black community leaders. However, no major downtown Detroit hotel would accommodate such a request, owing to the presence of blacks on the list of guests. Despite his standing within the community, Couzens was hard-pressed to find a venue fitting his needs until, after much negotiation, the YMCA offered to host the event. The Y was largely segregated, and few blacks had been able to use its facilities except through the direct intervention of an important patron. Access to theaters, public parks, hotels, swimming facilities and other accommodations—protected in theory by post–Civil War anti-discrimination laws—was frequently denied or restricted during much of the period of the Great Migration.

Traveling downtown in search of recreation or entertainment for residents of West Eight Mile was problematic. Black Bottom was not considered a family destination, but it did afford adult access to taverns, dance halls and live entertainment. There was very little for children to do, except go to the Main Public Library on Woodward Avenue and select movie houses, although some offered only balcony seating for blacks. Belle Isle was a popular public venue during the summer months, but on weekends and holidays, blacks and whites competed for baseball diamonds, picnic tables and prime beach spots, causing racial tension and occasional confrontation.

In 1937, State Senator Charles Diggs pushed a bill through Lansing to make it a misdemeanor to deny service on the basis of race, ethnicity or religion. Violators were subject to a twenty-five-dollar fine, fifteen days in jail or both. Drugstore lunch counters like Hechtman's and large restaurants like Greenfields's flouted the law and simply paid the fines.[109] In other establishments, denial of service came in many forms—asking black patrons to take their food on paper plates outside to eat, charging higher prices or simply delaying service. This is not to say that there were no restaurants willing to serve African Americans, but certainly for residents of West Eight Mile who were unfamiliar with the lay of the land, a casual visit downtown could turn into a humiliating experience.

After Higginbotham School was opened in 1928, Birdhurst took on a second life as a much-needed community center for area children. With limited funding from the City of Detroit but under the astute direction of Sheldon Johnson, the center made due through the volunteer efforts of members of the community and from students at Wayne State University to provide a number of enrichment activities for both children and adults. Classes were held in sewing, dancing, theatrics, music, painting, drawing, sculpting and storytelling. Depending on the weather and the time of year, physical activities—skipping rope, hopscotch, baseball, handball and basketball—were supervised on the old school grounds. In the 1930s, dances were held for adults, and Royal Oak Township residents across Eight Mile Road were naturally invited because the two communities were so intimately linked by history and culture. The dances became so popular that organizers—particularly Ida Brooks, Allen Jones and Parnell Allen—rented a hall, and the event became known as the 8 Mile Road Old Timers' Ball, which lasted many years.

DETROIT URBAN LEAGUE

The Detroit Urban League (DUL), an affiliate of the National Urban League, was founded in 1916 to address the growing needs of African Americans migrating from the South to Detroit. In the early years, particularly during World War I, daily trains arriving at the Michigan Central Depot would empty their passenger cars of southern migrants who, more often than not, were ignorant of Detroit's peculiarities. Volunteer members would meet the trains and provide the new arrivals with initial guidance. Invariably, these arriving individuals or families would need assistance locating housing, finding employment, registering children at school and gaining access to local healthcare facilities. Navigating this new environment was made less intimidating for migrants by mentors who knew the lay of the land and could steer individuals and families away from awkward or even dangerous predicaments within an intensely segregated city.

For the DUL, the West Eight Mile community existed as an island, a curious suburban experiment in self-help far away from the constant drama of the lower East Side ghetto. Social workers from downtown periodically visited and reported back to the main office the progress of the black enclave north of the city, which seemed to be barely subsisting on subdivided farmland. By the mid-1930s, John Dancy, the DUL's second director, was starting to pay more attention to the struggling community. Adults in the enclave were particularly stressed and were clearly in need of whatever outside relief could be provided by such an organization. In his 1966 memoirs, *Sand Against the Wind*, Dancy recalled:

> It became apparent that there was a need for an Urban League facility in the
> Eight Mile Road–Livernois area. The league rented a school building on
> the north side of Eight Mile and then set up programs which were thought

to be stimulating and purposeful to residents of both Royal Oak Township and the Detroit side of Eight Mile Road. Mrs. Eleanor Shamwell Griffen, who had just come to Detroit following her graduation with a Master's degree from Columbia University, was assigned by the League to conduct the program. Mrs. Griffen was a very enterprising young woman who not only had training in social work but was also well trained in music. She set about to develop club activities among the men and women. She also set up a home-and-garden club which busied itself with improving the homes and the grounds. Dilapidated homes began to take on a new look. Houses were painted, lawns were planted, schoolchildren began to dress more neatly, and some sections became especially attractive. Many little parties were planned for the children to acquaint them with various institutions like the library and the art institute. Mrs. Griffen took them on trips to Greenfield Village and on other sight-seeing tours so that they might be able to see some of the worthwhile things Detroit has to offer.[110]

With the success of this second new community center, the DUL decided to establish a more permanent presence in the West Eight Mile enclave. Fred Butzel, an attorney and businessman widely known for his community service and philanthropy, donated two lots on the west side of Northlawn. A gift of $10,000 from the McGregor Fund to construct a small building on the site helped to make the DUL's ambitious early plans a reality. About 1,500 people gathered in front of the new center at 20435 Northlawn, between Norfolk and Eight Mile Road, in 1937 for the DUL's center's dedication. Although it had an assembly room that could accommodate as many as 100 individuals, it was otherwise a small, efficient facility, with a room and bath for the caretaker, a little library and a very small kitchen. The dedication ceremony, held on the front lawn because of the size of the gathering, was highlighted by the presence and support of Joe Louis, Detroit's world heavyweight champion. After the ceremony, the jovial crowd filtered through the facility, imagining its possibilities.

The DUL staff had a good working relationship with their counterparts at Birdhurst Center, and to help redistribute the workload involved in managing all of the activities, Birdhurst transferred a number of clubs that had originated at the old school over to the new Northlawn facility. Mrs. Griffen began her tenure in the new environment by starting new music classes with high reported enrollments.

Even with both the Birdhurst and Detroit Urban League providing small outdoor play areas for the neighborhood children, a large playground/

Detroit Urban League Building, under renovation. *Author's collection.*

park was missing and badly needed. Acutely aware of the lack of recreation space to satisfy the needs of the local neighborhood children, Director Johnson presented to the City Plan Commission petitions signed by more than five hundred persons urging that a site in the very middle of the West Eight Mile community be designated a city park. The choice of the fifteen-acre tract—bounded by Cherrylawn, Chippewa, Wisconsin and Norfolk—was not without controversy, as twenty-two families would be forced to move from their homes on the tract if plans for the park were approved. In a contentious hearing before the commission, a large delegation of homeowners vigorously protested being thrown out of their homes. Nonetheless, believing that the needs of the larger community outweighed the rights of a group of contesting families, the commission voted unanimously to use its power of eminent domain to clear the tract of land for a public playground, to be named after local legend Joe Louis.

The drowning of a seven-year-old boy in a sand pit filled with rain water in the summer of 1948 was a great tragedy for the community. The sand pit was owned by Harry D'Achille, owner of D'Achille Trucking Sand Company, who was eventually cleared of criminal responsibility after his trial was delayed nine times. Neighbors had complained that the pit was a hazard, an accident waiting to happen—one that nonetheless attracted children because it was unfenced and there were no places around for black children to swim. The scene at the pit at the time of the drowning horrified onlookers as rescuers used giant grappling hooks normally used for construction to extract the boy's body from the hole.

Despite the drowning, D'Achille tried unsuccessfully to secure a circuit court injunction to restrain the city from interfering with his business. The extent of his callous disregard for human life—particularly for that of young children wandering too closely to his excavation sites—played out the following summer before Traffic Judge George T. Murphy. D'Achille was found guilty of maintaining a nuisance by permitting an open, water-filled sand pit on Eight Mile Road, between Greenfield and Stahelin. Judge Murphy fined D'Achille $250 and gave him a tongue lashing. He was also ordered to install a fence around the pit and to drain it.[111]

As a direct consequence of the tragedy and the court case, Sheldon Johnson petitioned the city for funds sufficient to construct an outdoor swimming pool to be located at the south end of Joe Louis Park. In 1956, following a second petition to the City Plan Commission, the Johnson Community Center, named after the man who had done so much to promote enrichment activities and social relations as recreation director at Birdhurst, would be constructed in such a way as to wrap completely

Johnson Recreation Center, Detroit. *Author's collection.*

around the existing outdoor pool. Now neighborhood children could swim year-round in the newly enclosed indoor pool.

After the construction of the Johnson Recreation Center, the Detroit Urban League scaled back its operations. As Dancy remembered, "It was felt that to maintain the Eight Mile Center would be a duplication of work, so the League decided to sell it. Certainly the department of recreation could do a bigger job, but we had fulfilled our function and believed that we had done much to raise the standard of living in that community."[112] In 2017, the 8 Mile Old Timers' Club entered into negotiations with the City of Detroit to purchase the old DUL building on Northlawn. Eventually, the building will serve as home to the club, as a community resource center and as a repository of all things historical as it relations to the West Eight Mile enclave.

"Ultimately, we are going to restore the building to its original condition," asserted Dwight Smith, president of the 8 Mile Old Timers' Club. "Once restored, the Old Timers' Club would use the facility for its meetings and associated gatherings. More importantly, we would like to see the building used as a community resource and activity center. The many uses for the center have not yet been fully articulated, but I would hope it would provide a much-needed employment center for teens and adults in the area who are struggling to find work."

Dwight Smith, president of 8 Mile Old Timers' Club. *Author's collection.*

Smith himself grew up in the West Eight Mile Road enclave, living at various times with his mother in Royal Oak Township and with his grandparents on the Detroit side. His grandparents were among the very early settlers of the area, having purchased a lot and built a home on Indiana Street near Eight Mile Road. Upon returning home in 1969 after a stint in the navy, Smith recalled how useful a DUL employment center would have been in helping him get relocated and find employment. However, if the club can obtain funding to fully renovate the building, future generations of West Eight Milers will have such a resource.

END OF AN ERA: THE JOHNSON RECREATION CENTER CLOSES

The Johnson Recreation Center was forced to close in 2006 following a thorough building inspection authorized by the city's General Services Division. The swimming pool, the centerpiece of the recreation center, was determined to be out of compliance with contemporary Building Safety Engineering Department standards and no longer cost-effective to maintain. The pool had been built around the previously existing outdoor pool. When the Johnson Recreation Center was built, the contractors wrapped the new face around the old structure and kept the old plumbing in place. Estimates to renovate the center with interior finishes and new equipment—and to replace its mechanical, electrical, fire-suppression and plumbing systems—came in at between $1 million and $2 million, a figure the City of Detroit was unable to fund due to budget constraints.

After remaining vacant and unused for a decade, except as a storage dump, the city put the property on the block, including the ten-acre Joe Louis Field on which the Recreation Center sat, for an asking price of $1 million. Almost immediately, controversy arose following the submission of a proposal by the University of Detroit Jesuit High School and Academy. The school offered to purchase both the Recreation Center and Higginbotham Elementary School for $500,000. Higginbotham School, located next door on a five-acre property, had been listed separately by the city for $500,000. The Catholic high school, located at Seven Mile and Cherrylawn, proposed further to demolish and abate Higginbotham, renovate the Recreation Center and construct three competitive soccer/lacrosse fields and one smaller competitive baseball field at the site. Two other proposals had been submitted to the city but were summarily rejected.

The crux of the controversy was access. Residents of the area, fearing permanent loss of a much-needed community resource, expressed serious reservations about the high school assuming ownership. At a community forum on March 23, 2017, at New Prospect Baptist Church, Father Theodore Munz, president of U-D Jesuit High School, and Kim Tandy, District 2 manager for the mayor's office, laid out the school's plans to redevelop the site. Despite immediate mixed reactions from residents and interested observers, the school received an important endorsement from the 8 Mile Road Old Timers' Club, which felt that there were sufficient safeguards in place to ensure that the West Eight Mile community would help to run the renovated center, have regular access to its facilities and be the recipient of U-D Jesuit–sponsored sports camps and other activities for neighborhood children.

THE CRYSTAL POOL: NO BLACKS, NO JEWS

The outdoor swimming pool at Joe Louis Park had become the summer locus of recreation for children in the area in the 1950s and '60s. Parents were delighted at the time to have such a facility, knowing as they did the very limited access to recreational swimming for blacks in metropolitan Detroit. The Detroit Parks Department managed the Central Community Center on Brewster Street downtown, but it was a long way to travel just to swim. After the high-rise Brewster-Douglass projects were completed, the Center admirably served the recreational needs of the more than ten thousand residents of the surrounding high-rises. But it rarely served the needs of the Eight Mile community, nor was it intended to do so.

The other main option was Belle Isle, even farther south, but racial incidents and confrontations had occurred on the island, so most West Eight Mile Road residents found the journey south not worth the effort. In 1943, such concerns proved justifiable when one incident in particular sparked a race riot with significant loss of life, major injuries and serious property damage.

Closer to home, African American teenagers were hearing on the street about a swimming facility open year-round and just down the road, a five-minute bike ride or ten minutes by foot traveling west along Eight Mile. The place could be the perfect complement, some thought, to the outdoor pool at Joe Louis Park, especially after it shut down at the end of the summer. Located on the northeast corner of Eight Mile and Greenfield Roads, the Crystal Pool was a segregated, membership-only indoor pool with two diving boards and a sixteen-foot diving tower hovering over ten feet depth of water. At the other end, where the bottom of the pool had sloped upward to create a wading area for smaller children and first-time swimmers—so long as they were white—kids could get acclimated to the water and splash around. A few of the more adventurous black teens in the area had bike ridden to Greenfield and attempted to breach the wall of segregation created by the security personnel but had not been successful. Legend has it that a few blacks had in fact been allowed in—or snuck in—depending on what version of the story one heard. The same story had whites either remove themselves from the area where blacks were swimming or confront and harass the black patrons. In either case, it was a place of mystery and ongoing curiosity for local black teens, a place about which parents could never seem to provide an adequate explanation for the stories of rejection.

Segregated pools like the Crystal Pool at the border of Oak Park and Detroit were the byproduct of two basic anxieties felt by whites at the time, according to Jeff Wiltse in *Contested Waters: A Social History of Swimming Pools*. Before the Great Migration, many whites discriminated against first-generation European immigrants on the basis of health concerns rooted in class distinctions. The immigrants were not only filthy and likely disease carriers but were ones with whom social—and of course physical—intercourse was prohibited. After the Great Migration, segregation policies and practices were racialized, and for white supremacists, contamination and miscegenation dovetailed into one fear: close contact with blacks, particularly where black men and white women might share space while wearing provocative clothing, threatened to "infect" the white race.

Frank Joyce, a prominent Detroit New Left civil rights and antiwar activist of the 1960s, recalled the final days of the Crystal Pool, as the owners decided to close its door rather than integrate the pool: "What I trace as my first overt political act was in the summer of 1960, I was driving down the infamous Eight Mile road, and I happened to notice a picket line, a demonstration that I couldn't really figure out what it was. But I was intrigued by it, so I made a U-turn on Eight Mile road and I came back, and I saw that it was a protest at a place called the Crystal Pool, and the protest was over the fact that the pool—remember this is 1960 in the North—that Crystal Pool denied admission to African Americans: it was a white-only public swimming pool in Oak Park, Michigan, in 1960. And I said, 'Well that's not right.' So I joined that picket line."[113] That night, Joyce's father watched local coverage of the protest on television, saw his teenage son on the picket line and kicked the teenage boy out of the house.

THE DUKE THEATER

Moviegoing was the rage in the 1940s, and a shopping trip downtown often included a few hours at one of a dozen elegant theaters watching a feature premiere or a first-run movie. But you didn't have to go downtown to see the latest movie. At their peak in the mid-1940s, there were 117 neighborhood theaters in Detroit, and after World War II, the West Eight Mile neighborhood, having waited so long, would have one it could call its very own, the Duke Theater at 10000 West Eight Mile and Wyoming.

The Duke Theater was named after jazz orchestra leader Duke Ellington, not John "Duke" Wayne, the Hollywood movie legend. Designed in Streamline Moderne style by Charles Agree, initial plans called for a 1941 or 1942 grand opening, but the material demands of the Second World

Duke Theater, Royal Oak Township. *Walter P. Reuther Library, Archives of Labor and Urban Affairs, Wayne State University.*

War delayed construction until 1946 at a cost of nearly $300,000. "The Duke," as it was simply called, was one link in a chain of twenty Detroit-based movie houses owned by Lew Wisper and Fred Wetsman. The theater opened in 1947 and adopted an experimental policy of presenting black vaudeville shows three nights a week, Sunday through Tuesday, catering to an exclusively black clientele. In addition, an amateur show was held on Wednesday nights. The only other theater in Detroit offering such stage shows was the Paradise Theater in Black Bottom, and it had already dropped amateur night, which had not proven a success.

Detroit's population peaked in the 1950 census at 1.86 million, and movie house popularity was a reflection of that growth. Over time, the stage shows disappeared, and such movie classics as *Moby Dick*, *12 Angry Men* and *The Hunchback of Notre Dame* filled the week's bill. Weekend matinee performances of horror and science fiction thrilled the neighborhood children, who were more than happy to sit through double features and cartoons as they munched popcorn and boxed candies. Ray Harryhausen's *20 Million Miles to Earth* and the *7th Voyage of Sinbad*, as well as Edward Cahn's *Invasion of the Saucer-Men* and *Creature with the Atom Brain*, were particular fan favorites, sometimes resulting in a line around the block to get in on Saturdays.

Duke Theater, just before the wrecking ball. *Randall Wilcox.*

Wisper and Wetsman could not have foreseen how market erosion due to television and suburbanization would produce steep declines in viewership in their Detroit neighborhood theaters. The trend was nationwide, as movie house attendance peaked at 90 million just after the war and dropped precipitously to 50 million by the early 1950s.

After "The Duke" closed its door in 1958, the building was repurposed as a bowling alley, the Starlite Lanes. When that business failed, the building was acquired by Robert Bartlett of Squire Bartlett Supply Company for use as a heating and cooling supply warehouse. In 2010, The Duke met the wrecking ball, and the eleven years of its existence as a movie mecca left indelible memories for a generation of West Eight Mile moviegoers.

BAKER'S KEYBOARD LOUNGE AND THE WEST EIGHT MILE ROAD JAZZ SCENE

Sitting at the northern tip of Detroit's "Avenue of Fashion" on Livernois near Eight Mile Road lies Baker's Keyboard Lounge, purportedly the oldest continuing jazz club in the United States. Clarence, the teenage son of Chris and Fannie Baker, conceived of the idea to augment his parents' sandwich deli business soon after it began operations in 1933. His strategy was to bring local jazz keyboard artists in to display their talents for an evening crowd after the deli closed for the day. Before very long, Clarence's evening business was outperforming his parents' daytime business, and the die was cast.

After his parents retired from the deli business, Clarence transformed the interior of the dual-use facility into the kind of intimate physical atmosphere that was ideal for both performing and listening. Even in the early years, the Lounge held its own against rival jazz clubs downtown, such as the 606 Horseshoe Lounge, Club Plantation, the Flame Show Bar and the Paradise Theater (now Orchestra Hall). Detroit was a magnet for the world's top jazz stars, including Sarah Vaughan, Duke Ellington, Count Basie, Billie Holiday, Dinah Washington, Ella Fitzgerald, John Coltrane, Miles Davis and Dave Brubeck. Baker's had no difficulty competing for these acts and was a particularly vital laboratory for local talent such as Earl Klugh, Alice Coltrane, Donald Byrd and Barry Harris. Kenny Burrell and Yusef Lateef, fresh out of Wayne State University's music department, explored new musical territory at Baker's.

Baker's Keyboard Lounge, Eight Mile and Livernois, Detroit. *Author's collection.*

Baker's Keyboard Lounge, delivery truck signage. *Author's collection.*

Major Holley. *Sophia Holley Ellis.*

After "urban renewal" wiped out most of the downtown jazz venues, Baker's continued to cultivate and showcase jazz talent in its ninety-nine-seat Art Deco establishment even through the city's most difficult periods. The club piano sitting atop the tiny stage today was donated by Art Tatum in 1954 as the great jazz pianist made Baker's his home during the final years of his life.

It was in this rarefied musical atmosphere that students and teachers in northwest Detroit began to explore jazz idioms as part of their academic musical instructions. Roland Harris, Tommy Flanagan, Barry Harris and Major Holley, for example, all established successful musical careers and national reputations in the process by cutting their teeth locally. Tommy Flanagan was born and raised in the Conant Garden neighborhood, the son of a postman. His first instrument of choice was the clarinet, but upon hearing Fats Waller perform with his parents at the Paradise Theater downtown, he realized instantly that his true medium was the piano. He began connecting with Barry Harris, with whom he shared a music teacher, and with Roland Harris, a fellow student at Northern.

Roland Harris began taking piano lessons at eleven, the same year he was admitted to Northern High School. Through his friendship with Tommy Flanagan, Hanna was introduced to the music of Art Tatum. During his summers, Hanna explored both jazz and blues at the Birdhurst Community Center, where Major "Mule" Holley was working as a teacher and counselor. Holley would become a world-renowned bassist, performing with Dexter Gordon, Charlie Parker, Ella Fitzgerald, Oscar Peterson and others.[114]

BRIGGS STADIUM OR MACK FIELD?

In Detroit, the Tigers of the 1940s were an attractive entertainment option; tickets were cheap and the team was competitive. A box seat cost $2.50, reserve seats were $1.75, general admission was $1.20 and bleacher seats were just $0.60. The Tigers had won the pennant in 1940 and the 1945 World Series with such fan favorites as Hank Greenberg and Hal Newhauser. But there were no black players on the roster, and that was by design.

Walter O. Briggs, the sole owner of the team from 1935 to 1952, had his own ideas how to run a professional ball team, and unlike all the other major-league teams save Boston, no black player would ever enter the clubhouse under his watch.

Briggs was otherwise an all-American success story. The son of immigrants, he was brought up in poverty in Ypsilanti, Michigan. In classic Horatio Alger style, he lifted himself up by the bootstraps to become a multimillionaire through, in the words of his great-grandson Harvey Briggs, "hard work, acute business sense, and ruthless competitiveness."[115] Briggs Manufacturing was a major automobile supplier to Ford, Chrysler, Packard and many others. During World War II, his factories quickly converted to

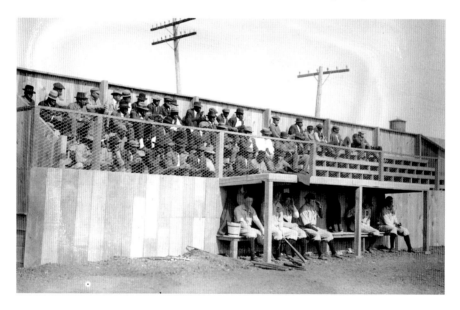

African American baseball spectators sit in segregated section above Detroit players' dugout at Navin Field (later Briggs Stadium) in Detroit. *Walter P. Reuther Library, Archives of Labor and Urban Affairs, Wayne State University.*

war production, building parts for the B26 and the A20 bombers as well as producing trucks, tank hulls, ambulance bodies and other stamped steel and aluminum products for the war effort.

His various factories employed thousands of African Americans, but they were principally restricted to jobs in the foundry and the paint shop or to menial jobs such as sweeping the floors or bathroom cleanup. When it came to the Detroit Tigers, the phrase around the clubhouse was "No Jigs with Briggs."

It was not until 1958, after Walter O. Briggs's death, that the Tigers signed a black utility player, Ozzie Virgil Sr., the first Dominican to play in Major League Baseball. The Tigers would be the second-to-last team to place a black player on its roster and the very last team to sign a black player to a contract. It would take until 1961 before the Tigers would elevate a black player, Jake Wood Jr., from its own minor-league system.

In 1919, the same year Walter O. Briggs was brought into the front office as a part owner of the Tigers, the Detroit Stars of the national Negro League was formed. Tenny Blount and Rube Foster, the original owners of the Stars, arranged to play their games at historic Mack Park. Located about four miles north of the downtown area, the park was located in the heart of the city's German community, a community not particularly receptive to blacks living or recreating within their neighborhood. And for Detroit Stars fans from the West Eight Mile Road community, getting to Mack Road was as problematic as getting to Michigan and Trumbull. The quickest route was Eight Mile to Woodward, Woodward to Mack and Mack to the Fairfield Avenue. Built to seat six thousand fans in a single-decked timber-built structure, the park was as intimate as one could imagine for a ballgame. With such stellar performers as Joe "Prince" Henry, Ted "Double Duty" Radcliffe and Norman "Turkey" Stearnes, it was easy to understand why the Stars enjoyed winning seasons every year but two, although the team could never quite pull off a championship. "Turkey" Stearnes, however, was a head above most of the players he shared the field with; some observers would claim that he was the best player of his era. He finished his career with 3,662 plate appearances, 176 home runs and a career batting average of .344. Ironically, Stearns made so little money playing the game he loved that he was forced to work a factory job just to make ends meet—at one of Walter O. Briggs's factories, no less.

On July 7, 1929, a double-header was scheduled between the Stars and the Kansas City Monarchs. Heavy rains the night before made the field unplayable, but a tactic used elsewhere to remove standing water was tried.

Aftermath of the fire at Mack Field, 1929. *Walter P. Reuther Library, Archives of Labor and Urban Affairs, Wayne State University.*

Gasoline was poured on the infield with the expectation that, once lit, all the standing water would evaporate. Unfortunately, possibly owing to gas cans leaking from the parking lot to the field, flames skipped under the bleachers, causing scores of fans to jump from the back of the grandstands, a fall of about thirty feet. Panic set in as the fire spread to other sections, and more injuries sent dozens of fans to area hospitals with lacerations, contusions and broken bones. Fortunately, no one was killed, but 220 people were injured, and Mack Park, as a Negro League venue, was no more. The rest of the season was played at Dequindre Park. The following year, and for six years thereafter, the Stars played at Hamtramck Stadium before returning to Dequindre Park in 1937 for a final season.

Conclusion

FROM SWEAT EQUITY TO RACIAL JUSTICE

H istory is a wheel, observed sixth-century Roman philosopher Boethius, and as the wheel spins, good fortune follows bad and no amount of human longing or effort can alter the ups and downs of fate. African Americans, however, have reason to wonder if fate, in its perversity, has put a finger on the wheel. Despite grindingly slow progress in overcoming barriers to racial justice and social equality in housing, education, transportation, employment, healthcare and public accommodations, new barriers to full civic participation continue to be erected. Lawmakers—Republican, Democrat and Independent—have put forth proposals to address past inequities and new issues as they arise.

REGIONAL PLANNING

Strategies to reduce racial and economic inequalities and improve the region's ability to compete took on added emphasis after the events of 1967 and became the focus of local and regional governments, if in some cases reluctantly. In 1968, the Southeast Michigan Council of Governments (SEMCOG) was created as a regional planning agency to address issues of transportation, water, air quality, housing and land use. It evolved out of predecessor organizations such as the Detroit Metropolitan Planning Commission, which dates back to the 1940s, and the Transportation and Land Use (TALUS), which originated in the early 1960s. A group calling itself the Committee of 100 formulated the mission of the organization and invited volunteer representatives from various public institutions—cities, villages, townships, school districts, community colleges and universities—based in Livingston, Macomb, Monroe, Oakland, St. Clair, Washtenaw and Wayne Counties.

One of SEMCOG's major responsibilities is regional transportation planning, and in 1974, the organization received its federal Metropolitan Planning Organization (MPO) status. The concept of an MPO is that local rather than federal officials have a better understanding of how to administer federal funding for transportation and land use.[116] In the years following, continued waves of white flight decimated Detroit's population and tax base, and Southeast Michigan became among the most racially segregated regions in the United States.

These dramatic demographic shifts have public policy implications for SEMCOG's use of transportation funding. In 2003, the faith-based citizens group Metropolitan Organizing Strategy Enabling Strength (MOSES), the City of Ferndale and the transportation advocacy group Transportation Riders United filed suit in Wayne County Circuit Court against SEMCOG's alleged discriminatory practices. The lawsuit claimed that SEMCOG discriminated against the poor, minorities and disabled people who rely on the region's inadequate system of public transportation. The fifty-one-member SEMCOG executive committee, which controls hundreds of millions of federal tax dollars and is largely controlled by suburban governments, gives too much consideration, the suit alleged, to building roads for people who drive and live in the largely white and wealthy outer suburbs. From a purely economic point of view, framed in language fiscal conservatives would understand, suburban sprawl is the direct consequence of massive governmental financial intrusion into free markets.[117]

Race and economic status, plaintiffs' attorneys argued, were at the heart of the issue. Each governmental unit had one vote, no matter their size. Thus, the pattern of representation in SEMCOG was set by the historical pattern of segregation. In 2003, the SEMCOG executive committee (EC) was dominated by representatives from newer, more remote communities. SEMCOG's bylaws allocated votes in its fifty-one-member Executive Committee disproportionate to the populations it served: Livingston County, four; Macomb County, seven; Monroe County, four; Oakland County, nine; St. Clair County, four; Washtenaw County, four; Wayne County (not including Detroit) nine; City of Detroit, three; and others (bloc chairs, governor, regional), three. Dr. Joseph Grengs of the University of Michigan's School of Urban Planning stated in an affidavit prepared for the suit, "The three most over-represented jurisdictions are Livingston, Monroe, and St. Clair Counties. If the same total of seats were redistributed on the EC based on population, each of these counties would receive one vote, instead of the four votes each is presently allocated. The city of Detroit is by far the most under-represented. If the same total of seats were redistributed based on population Detroit would have nine seats, not three."[118]

The 2000 census indicated Livingston County had fewer than 1,000 African Americans. Macomb, Monroe and St. Clair Counties were less than 3 percent black. Detroit, on the other hand, was 82 percent black; the majority of Wayne County's 200,000 other blacks lived in inner-ring suburbs. Dr. Grengs's analysis suggested "a strong and statistically significant relationship between race and representation."[119] Voting consistently and disproportionately on outer suburban highway projects, while essentially neglecting the region's public transit system that serves the region's poor, minorities and disabled people, the executive committee engaged in discriminatory practices in direct violation of the Elliot-Larson Civil Rights Act, which prohibits discrimination against persons with disabilities, and the state constitutional guarantees of equal protection and the right to travel freely.

On October 4, 2004, Wayne County Circuit Court judge John H. Gillis Jr. dismissed the lawsuit, in part because the plaintiffs lacked standing, in that the City of Detroit was not a party to the suit. Detroit had, in fact, declined being co-plaintiff after its own attorneys concluded that SEMCOG had not violated state civil rights law. Furthermore, despite SEMCOG's failure to refute plaintiffs' statistical evidence showing the underrepresentation of Detroit and its inner-ring suburbs in executive committee decision-making, Judge Gillis ruled that plaintiffs failed to show how the committee's structure "burdened African Americans more harshly than members of other racial groups."[120] After the court ruling, SEMCOG implemented a two-tiered voting system. The first uses a one-vote/one government arrangement; the second bases committee representation on population. Any measure before the committees must pass both; if it lacks sufficient support by either group, the measure dies.

The formation of SEMCOG was not the only attempt to address regional issues in a comprehensive fashion after the urban unrest of the late 1960s. At The Option Process (TOP) conference convened in Detroit on May 23, 1972, by Housing and Urban Development secretary George Romney,

Governor William Milliken and Mayor Roman Gribbs, a task force was appointed by the governor to conduct a thorough examination of problems in the metropolitan Detroit area and to recommend effective solutions. The thirty-six-member task force comprised representatives of government, industry, labor and citizens' groups and was chaired by John Mogk and Richard Simmons, both of Wayne State University.

Nine months later, the task force submitted its report to Governor Milliken, with a number of specific recommendations. The first was to substantially strengthen the role and function of SEMCOG "to meet the compelling need for improved coordination of regionally significant governmental services, functions and resources in the seven counties of Southeast Michigan."[121] The remaining recommendations included revisions to state and federal law affecting funding chiefly for transportation, housing, healthcare and education.

While the governor and a handful of legislators remained interested in such regional planning, the lack of local municipal and suburban support spelled doom for any of the measures recommended by the task force. Mayor Roman Gribbs, though very interested in the report's finding, had decided not to run for reelection in 1974. As a lame-duck chief executive, he would have neither the time nor political influence to guide the package of recommendations through to implementation. His successor, Coleman A. Young, showed no inclination to provide the kind of leadership necessary to rally regional support.

Another proposal supporting regional planning surfaced two years later when House Speaker William Ryan and Representative Philip Mastin introduced House Bill 5527, known as the Local Cooperation Act, on July 22, 1975. Essentially, this bill would have established a new regional planning agency to replace SEMCOG. This new Southeast Michigan Planning and Development Agency would have legal authority to coordinate and hold accountable publicly funded special purpose regional agencies. The bill died in the Urban Affairs Committee.

The TOP task force and the Local Cooperation Act represented missed opportunities to develop a long-term master plan for marshalling and coordinating regional resources to address such important issues as land use, economic inequalities, suburban sprawl, segregated housing, mass transit and equal educational opportunities.

DESEGREGATING THE
DETROIT PUBLIC SCHOOL SYSTEM

By any measure, Detroit remains among the most segregated cities in the United States.[122] The forced segregation of African Americans into neighborhoods of substandard housing, limited employment opportunities and poor transportation has led to significant social and economic consequences for residents in those neighborhoods. Another consequence of immense importance to Detroiters has been the long-term impact of forced segregation on the quality of public education. Without the same or similar property tax structure that its wealthier, nearby suburbs enjoy, educational funding for Detroit Public Schools remains deficient in terms of providing a comparable learning environment. Following suit by the NAACP in 1970, Federal District Court judge Stephen J. Roth found that housing and school segregation were essentially interdependent, caused in part by policies such as restrictive residential covenants, as well as the coordinated practices of local banks and real estate brokers. Judge Roth's remedy, in essence, was to create a regional school integration plan involving fifty-three metropolitan school districts.

The goal of the judicial remedy was not only to integrate Detroit schools but also to discourage further white flight. Had the ruling been restricted to enforcing busing solely within the city of Detroit, the cure might well have been worse than the disease: Detroit's remaining middle-class whites would more than likely flee to the suburbs rather than permit their children to be bused across town.

On appeal, the Sixth Circuit affirmed Roth's remedy, based on discriminatory school policies, but chose not to address the issue of interdependence between housing discrimination and school segregation. Furthermore, owing to a technical defect in the Roth directive, the appeals court prohibited the state from purchasing 295 buses to effect the implementation of the inter-district busing plan.

Meanwhile, the State of Michigan and the affected Detroit suburbs jointly appealed to the United States Supreme Court. Arguing that the suburban communities had formed no policies that discriminated against black children—ironically, housing policies made *that* unnecessary—the high court reversed the decision of the appeals court and remanded the case to the district court to devise and implement a Detroit-only solution to segregation.

Had *Milliken v. Bradley* approved the regional school integration plan, according to John Mogk, Professor Emeritus of Wayne State University

School of Law, "white flight would have been discouraged and Metro Detroit would not be the most segregated region in the U.S. today."[123] The court's final ruling, however, would have both local and national implications. Locally, many of the remaining white residents would flee to the suburbs to avoid having their children bused across town to previously segregated, and in some cases, dilapidated school buildings in the interest of fulfilling court-mandated racial integration of Detroit schools.

Nationally, advocates of school desegregation in other metropolitan areas could no longer expect court remedies to redress school segregation as the result of government policies.

TAX BASE SHARING

In his State of the State address on January 14, 1976, Republican Governor William Milliken proposed a strategy to address the tax-based inequality between municipalities in the seven-county area of southeastern Michigan. The new program would redistribute tax dollars from expanding communities within the region to Detroit and other stagnating cities, with the anticipated collateral benefit of curbing white flight.[124]

Tax base sharing is not a new concept, but it has gained only minimal acceptance as a local government finance tool. The theory underlying tax base sharing is not complicated. So long as public services such as police and fire, local infrastructure and parks are dependent on local property wealth and retail and industrial development, tax sharing helps to maintain metropolitan stability in three distinct ways.[125] First, it reduces fiscal disparities between communities and creates social equity. The equity problem is most critical in central cities and inner-ring suburbs where concentrated poverty, abandoned properties and declining populations produce greater needs due to a devastated tax base and declining state and federal support for urban programs. Those parts of a region with a growing tax base, it is argued, are less likely to have the same social needs as areas where the tax base is uncertain or declining.

A second suggested benefit of tax base sharing is that it reduces competition for tax base. A business intending to locate within a region might encourage competition by pitting the public resources of one community against another through tax abatements and other tax-advantaged inducements. In such a competitive environment, a business is far more likely to look at its bottom line than its social responsibility.

A third suggested benefit of tax base sharing is that it directs more efficient land-use decisions. As urban sprawl occurs and new communities develop, large debt burdens in terms of streets, sewers, parks and school stand in sharp contrast to fully developed communities—with existing infrastructure—that become significantly underutilized.

Five years before Governor Milliken delivered his State of the State address, the Minnesota legislature adopted a regional tax base sharing system for the Twin Cities metropolitan area, known generally as the "fiscal disparities program." Under the program, 40 percent of the growth of the commercial and industrial tax base in the metro area goes into a shared pool. Communities with a smaller per capita property value compared to the metro average get a larger distribution, while communities with a larger per capita property value get a smaller distribution. The key feature is that local jurisdictions share a portion of the future growth in the tax base rather than the existing tax base. This means that, initially, tax base sharing has little effect on a region. As the region grows and prospers, the shared base also grows and becomes relatively more important. Since only 40 percent of the growth in the commercial-industrial tax is shared, the bulk of all future growth remains in the local jurisdiction.[126]

The experience of the Twin Cities metropolitan area has demonstrated over the past forty-five years that tax base sharing need not create a new layer of government because the contribution and distribution formulae are predetermined and made a part of the tax base sharing agreement itself. Nor does tax base sharing alter local decision-making authority. Local jurisdictions continue to independently set or restrict spending priorities just as they have always done.

Tax base sharing has its critics.[127] Some wealthy suburban communities have complained that it takes millions of dollars from their budgets and subsidizes poorer communities that don't account for how they use the money. Another argument suggests that any perceived revenue surplus created by local business and industry should be seen as compensation to local residents for undesirable—and immeasurable—costs (pollution, traffic congestion and so on) created by those companies. The very existence of zoning laws is evidence that business and industry are a necessary evil. The most frequent criticism is that tax base sharing creates "winners" and "losers." Using historic growth patterns, critics in richer districts worry they are already "losers" even though it is future—and therefore unpredictable—commercial-industrial growth that is shared. However, in Minnesota, where there was no dearth of such critics in the very beginning, computer runs were developed that showed the projected amount of tax base cities would actually gain. Most of the inner and developing middle-class suburbs were potential recipients. When these suburban officials realized that tax based sharing was likely to increase their tax base and stabilize their fiscal situation, they became supporters. As one legislator told Myron Orfield, "Before the [simulated tax base sharing] runs, tax base sharing was communism, afterward it was 'pretty good policy.'"[128]

Nonetheless, like the regional planning initiatives before it, Governor Milliken's proposal never gained traction. A combined failure of leadership in both Detroit and Lansing, as well as staunch suburban resistance, resulted in not a single House or Senate bill promoting tax base sharing for southeastern Michigan. A 2000 study looked at tax base sharing across the United States and concluded that some form of tax base or revenue sharing between central city and suburbs was common in nearly every one of the twenty-seven major metropolitan areas. However, Detroit was a prime example of a major urban center where there was virtually no evidence of sharing the burden.

COALITIONS AND POLITICAL IMPROVISATION

Absent a top-down master plan to address issues of regional equity, local groups and organizations have explored various options to achieve bottom-up reform. Following the Twelfth Street Riot in Detroit in 1967, the very stability of the city was at stake. After the last fires were quenched, the National Guard departed and the cleanup begun, everyone living or working in the city knew that the present environment was a powder keg. Many residents of the poorest neighborhoods were drifting toward radicalization, and there were many militant organizations like Uhuru, Black Guards and Black Panthers actively recruiting. The disaffection with the failed strategies of the liberal white city administration, as well as the civil rights leaders of the black middle class, was only surpassed by the stepped-up law-and-order agenda of the racially conservative whites.

Many more residents felt that lack of biracial communication was the crux of the problem. In the weeks and months to follow, disparate groups began to communicate with a sense of urgency. Polish and African Americans came together, for example, to form the Black Polish Conference, a group of more than four thousand citizens that offered a forum to improve communication. "Blacks and Poles share many of the same problems and that by working together, we can overcome these problems without losing our ethnic identity," observed the writer of one Polish Conference report.[129] Blacks and whites had also come together to form an organization known as Focus Hope. Cofounded by Father William Cunningham, Father Jerome Fraser and Eleanor Josaitis, Focus Hope worked closely with fifty other individuals active in the civil rights movement to try and rebuild the city into a diverse community living and working together. Several other activists were attempting to reinvigorate the "block clubs" of the previous decade, hoping to provide a convenient meeting ground for both black and white residents who might otherwise have some difficulty relating to each other easily.[130]

The Cavanagh administration was quick to take note of these working coalitions and created its own committee, the Mayor's Development Team, to address the urban crisis by coordinating all public agencies and establishing a blueprint for the city's redevelopment. At the same time, Governor Romney and Mayor Cavanagh asked business executive Joseph L. Hudson Jr. to head up a committee made up of civic, business, labor and civil rights leaders to marshal private as opposed to public funds to rebuild the city. As Hudson described it, "When 39 community leaders joined together to form New Detroit in August, 1967, we were really pioneering new ground. An urban coalition had never been formed before. There was no master plan, and no relevant body of knowledge to guide us."[131]

Fifty years after the worst civil rebellion in the city's history, we are left to ask where we are as a city and as a region. Historically, in one small corner of the region, the West Eight Mile African American enclave has become the epitome of historic racial discrimination. It was directly affected by discriminatory practices in the areas of housing, employment, education, transportation, healthcare and public accommodations. These practices permeated the political, legal, economic and social environment from the federal to the local level, with little public dissent.

Addressing the long-term effects of the general discrimination on the individuals and on the community is impossible without efforts directed at systemic changes (regional planning, tax base sharing and school desegregation are but a few proposed examples). Piecemeal and disconnected efforts tend to be ineffective in preventing malignant problems long in the making. Factoring in counterforces and efforts from extremist groups—white supremacists and separatists, neo-Nazis, neo-Confederates, racist skinheads, certain Christian identity groups and more—into the equation of success and failure makes the outcome, if any, more difficult to obtain.

At the center of change are the residents of the West Eight Mile community, who have displayed from the beginning an inestimable measure of self-reliance and resilience. Within and outside this neighborhood enclave, the Birwood Wall remains a potent symbol of the many other barriers residents have had to overcome in order to fully participate in the American experience.

In the years following construction of the wall, new neighbors came, old neighbors left and the wall itself became less visible to individuals passing along Birwood or Mendota. Houses went up on both sides of the wall, as did backyard garages and chain link fencing between yards. Bushes and hedges became overgrown, making a viewing of the wall nearly impossible, except for one small patch of grass on the first block of Birwood off Eight Mile. A small children's playground—with a set of swings and monkey bars but not much else—jutted out from the street looking south. Through the efforts of Alfonso Wells, a local resident and political activist, and the Detroit Pistons organization, the little park was expanded and now included a covered picnic area and multiple basketball courts and play areas.

Alfonso Wells was a large, physically imposing man, by all accounts a gentle giant. Born on May 12, 1912, in Pittsylvania County, Virginia, Alfonso had a choice of working the tobacco fields or the coal mines. He chose the coal mines, and for any friend who feared failing the employment physical, he would stand in for them, as physicals were administered away from the employment office.

When he came to Detroit just before the war, he worked in the auto plants, later at Willow Run, and met and married Carmen Lopez, who was living in the housing projects on Birwood during the war. Alfonso moved Carmen and her two sons, Carlos and Benjamin, to a house he had purchased on Ilene. The house was ramshackle, like a lot of the prewar structures built by the early residents of the area. He and the boys dug a trench in the backyard, installed underground pipes and connected the house to city water to add at least that modern convenience to the house. Soon they would move to Griggs—and a little closer to the wall.

Over the next several years, Alfonso and Carmen adopted two boys and fostered 125 babies who were otherwise waiting to be adopted at a Methodist home for pregnant girls on Six Mile Road. Alfonso was a staunch advocate for senior citizens in the neighborhood, obtaining grants to rehabilitate homes for these needy individuals. He was also a political activist, driving through the West Eight Mile community using a loudspeaker that he duct-taped to the roof of his car (and later a van), endorsing various candidates and

Mural depicting Alfonso Wells on Birwood Wall, located in Alfonso Wells Memorial Playground. *Author's collection.*

Alfonso Wells, community activist. *Family of Alfonso Wells.*

promoting any issue that he felt served the needs of his community. He enlisted his sons and other neighborhood kids to go door to door handing out handbills as well.

Five years after his death, a successful petition drive resulted in the city naming the park after this beloved and widely respected neighborhood giant. The Alfonso Wells Playground now draws kids to the park every day to play; it draws others, from much farther away, to get a view of the Birwood Wall, where it is most fully exposed.[132]

In an effort to transform the wall into something more uplifting than a memorial to segregation, in 2006 artist Chazz Miller designed a mural for its most highly visible section, at the back of Alfonso Wells Memorial Playground. The mural became a reality on a cloudless Saturday in June, when the nonprofit Motor City Blightbusters brought along nearly one hundred artists and community volunteers to the playground to execute Miller's vision. One section portrays Sojourner Truth leading children through the Underground Railroad. On another, Rosa Parks boards the bus in Montgomery, Alabama, where she refused to surrender her seat to a white rider, helping to precipitate the Montgomery Bus Boycott. Other sections of the wall celebrate African American culture, venerate the civil rights movement and even evoke bitter memories of the segregationist South with one portrayal of a Klansman in hot pursuit of a slave.

The murals at this section of the Birwood Wall have inspired Green Industries, a jobs program of Cass Community Services, to manufacture coasters featuring photographic reproductions on recycled glass (from a Guardian Glass business) framed with repurposed wood from demolished homes. The coasters not only provide jobs for people with significant barriers to employment but have the added benefit of stimulating a discussion about race in Detroit.[133]

The colorful murals of more recent creation depict moments in the civil rights struggle, such as Alfonso Wells, who went door to door drumming up support for one neighborhood project or another.

Top: Mural depicting man blowing bubbles for children in playground. *Author's collection.*

Bottom: Mural of Rosa Parks, the "First Lady of the Civil Rights Movement," as she prepares to board a bus in Montgomery, Alabama. *Author's collection.*

Top: Three-dimensional mural of the bus on which Rosa Parks refused to surrender her seat to a white person, thus launching the Montgomery Bus Boycott and the civil rights movement. *Author's collection.*

Bottom: Hovering presence of shrouded Klansman on mural in Alfonso Wells Memorial Playground. *Author's collection.*

Top: Teresa Moon, president of Eight Mile Homeowner's Association, standing by the mural in Alfonso Wells Memorial Playground. *Author's collection.*

Bottom: The Wall in Alfonso Wells Memorial Playground. *Author's collection.*

Teresa Moon, sixty-eight, resides in a modest bungalow on Griggs Street, directly across from the Alfonso Wells Playground. She reflects on the sixty years she has lived in the neighborhood. "The Wall has been there for nearly my entire life. There are new families moving in and old families moving out, but the one constant has been the Wall. It's important that we use the Wall to educate our kids. They can't be allowed to lose sight of its history, its meaning, what it was erected for and what it represents. You always have someone or something standing in your way, and you have to learn to stand up for yourself. With that said, it's a balancing act. You can't spend your whole life dwelling on the past or rest on your accomplishments. There's still a lot to be done to make sure everybody has a chance to achieve their dreams and not let something like a wall stand in their way."[134]

NOTES

Introduction

1. Avery, *Walk Quietly through the Night and Cry Softly*, 148.
2. "A Short History of the Oak Grove A.M.E. Church," Oak Grove AME Church Archives.
3. Ruth Rosa Green, "Neighborhood Was a Melting Pot," *Detroit Free Press*, October 10, 1988, 16A.
4. Burneice Avery, "A Mine Disaster Sparked Move to Detroit," *Detroit Free Press*, January 26, 1987, 14A.
5. "Map of Detroit Annexation 1806–1926," detroitography.com.
6. Avery, "Mine Disaster."
7. Dan Austin and J.C. Reindl, "Once Crown Jewel, Detroit Train Station Now Symbol of Ruin," *Detroit Free Press*, December 26, 2013, 2A.
8. Levine, *Internal Combustion*, 58–59.
9. Anderson, *Education of Blacks in the South*.
10. See Williams, *Detroit*.
11. Berman, *Metropolitan Jews*, 107.
12. Dancy, *Sand Against the Wind*, 57.
13. Ibid.
14. "Short History of the Oak Grove A.M.E. Church."
15. Harris-Slaughter, *Our Lady of Victory*, 91.
16. Ibid., 51–53.
17. Ibid., 62.
18. Ibid., 215–16.

19. Waxman, *Seekers and Creators of Community Change*, vol. 1, 255.
20. Ibid.
21. Avery, "Eight Mile Road."
22. Ibid., *Walk Quietly through the Night and Cry Softly*, 111.
23. Mirel, *Rise and Fall of an Urban School System*, 201.
24. Avery, "Eight Mile Road."
25. Moon, *Untold Tales, Unsung Heroes*, 73–74.
26. Ibid.
27. Mike Wilkinson, "Michigan's Segregated Past—and Present (Told in 9 Interactive Maps)," *Bridge*, August 8, 2017, www.bridgemi.com/public-sector/michigans-segregated-past-and-present-told-9-interactive-maps.
28. Berman, *Metropolitan Jews*, 106.
29. Avery, *Walk Quietly through the Night and Cry Softly*, 29.

Chapter 1

30. Dr. Mark Hyman's blog, "How Social Networks Control Your Health," drhyman.com/blog/2012/01/31/how-social-networks-control-your-health.
31. Seeley, *History of Oakland County Michigan*, 28–29.
32. *Michigan History Magazine* 2, no. 1, "Historical News, Notes and Comment" (January 1918): 43.
33. Peterson, *Planning the Home Front*, 261.
34. Ibid.

Chapter 2

35. Daines, *Be It Ever So Tumbled*, 4.
36. Capeci, *Race Relations in Wartime Detroit*, 10.
37. Daines, *Be It Ever So Tumbled*, 32–33.
38. Ibid., 50–51.
39. Quoted in Alan Clive's *State of War: Michigan in World War II* (Ann Arbor: University of Michigan Press, 1979), 2.
40. Peterson, *Planning the Home Front*, 259–60.
41. Waxman, *Seekers and Creators of Community Change*, 163.
42. Ibid.
43. Ibid.
44. Royal Oak Township, royaloaktwp.com.

45. Peterson, *Planning the Home Front*, 261.
46. Daines, *Be It Ever So Tumbled*, 30–31.
47. Fine, *Expanding the Frontiers of Civil Rights*, 116.
48. Berman, *Metropolitan Jews*, 110.
49. Ibid.
50. Ibid.
51. Capeci, *Race Relations in Wartime Detroit*, 21.
52. Ibid., 22.
53. Brown, *Social Psychology*, 730.
54. Fine, *Violence in the Model City*, 17.

Chapter 3

55. Levine, *Internal Combustion*, 12.
56. DETROITography, detroitography.com.
57. Washington, *Negro in Detroit*, 1.
58. Levine, *Internal Combustion*, 71–72, 84.
59. Dancy, *Sand Against the Wind*, 133–36.
60. Tim Worstall, "The Story of Henry Ford's $5 a Day Wages: It's Not What You Think," *Forbes*, March 4, 2012, forbes.com/sites/timworstall/2012/03/04/the-story-of-henry-fords-5-a-day-wages-its-not-what-you-think.
61. Levine, *Internal Combustion*, 21–26.
62. Ibid., 17.
63. Lacey, *Ford*, 341–56.
64. Bates, "Double V for Victory," 17–39.
65. Waxman, *Seekers and Creators of Community Change*, vol. 1, 248.
66. Sugrue, *Origins of the Urban Crisis*, 120–21.

Chapter 4

67. Interview, Sophia Holley Ellis, June 14, 2018.
68. Daines, *Be It Ever So Tumbled*, 35.
69. Ibid., 37.
70. Detroit, the History and Future of the Motor City, "George Washington Carver Elementary School," http://detroit1701.org/Carver%20Elementary%20School.html.

71. Detroit Transit History, "DSR School-Run Mystery Photo," detroittransithistory.info/Misc/DSRSchoolPhoto.html.

72. Waxman, *Seekers and Creators of Community Change*, vol. 2, 122.

73. Interview, Gloria Butler, July 14, 2018.

74. William K. Stevens, "U.S. Pressing School Integration in a Detroit Suburb," *New York Times*, June 13, 1975, nytimes.com/1975/06/13/archives/us-pressing-school-integration-in-a-detroit-suburb.html.

75. *United States v. School Dist. of Ferndale*, Mich., 460 F. Supp. 352 (E.D. Mich. 1978), law.justia.com/cases/federal/district-courts/FSupp/460/352/2093281.

76. Excerpted from *Growing Up in Ferndale* by Thomas Coleman, with permission of author, tomcoleman.us/Ferndale/book-final.pdf.

77. Mirel, *Rise and Fall of an Urban School System*, 193.

78. Ibid.

79. Ibid., 217.

80. Ibid., 258–59.

81. Wolf, *Trial and Error*, 283–301.

82. Barry M. Frankin, "Achievement, Race and Urban School Reform in Historical Perspectives: Three Views from Detroit," *Education Research and Perspectives* 31, no. 2 (2004): 16–21.

83. Fine, *Violence in the Model City*, 52.

84. Harding, Kelley and Lewis, *We Changed the World*, 171–72.

85. Office of the County Clerk, Wayne County Election Commission, Certified Election Results.

86. Detroiturbex, "Highland Park High School/Junior College/Career Academy," detroiturbex.com/content/schools/hphs.

87. *Detroit News*, "College on Clear Path," December 18, 1960, 3A.

88. Peter J. Stanlis, Letter to the Editor, *Wyandotte Tribune*, November 24, 1960, 8.

89. Russell Kirk, "The Community College Boondoggle," *National Review*, December 17, 1960, 379.

90. Don Beck, "Local Opposition Led to Defeat of Community College Measure," *Detroit Free Press*, June 5, 1961, 36.

Chapter 5

91. *Detroit Free Press*, "Neighborhood Was a Melting Pot," October 10, 1988, 16A.

92. Daines, *Be It Ever So Tumbled*, 19.

93. Nick DiUlio, "Detroit Most Expensive U.S. Metro Area for Car Insurance," Insurance Quotes, September 11, 2014, www.insurancequotes.com/auto/most-expensive-metropolitan-areas-for-car-insurance.

94. JC Reindl, "Free Press Report: Why Does Auto Insurance in Detroit Cost So Much?" *Detroit Free Press*, May 8, 2017, www.freep.com/story/news/local/michigan/detroit/2017/05/06/detroit-car-insurance-expensive-cost/101374948.

95. Dancy, *Sand Against the Wind*, 108.

96. Capeci, *Race Relations in Wartime Detroit*, 67.

97. Detroit Transit History, detroittransithistory.info.

Chapter 6

98. Harris-Slaughter, *Our Lady of Victory*, 65.

99. Dancy, *Sand Against the Wind*, 150.

100. Capeci, *Race Relations in Wartime Detroit*, 37–41.

101. Ibid., 37.

102. Kellogg African American Healthcare Project, Bentley Historical Library, University of Michigan, www.med.umich.edu/haahc.

103. Moon, *Untold Tales, Unsung Heroes*, 313.

104. Ibid., 288–89.

105. Washington, *Negro in Detroit*, 180.

106. Dancy, *Sand Against the Wind*, 145.

107. Waxman, *Seekers and Creators of Community Change*, vol. 1, 113.

Chapter 7

108. Interview, Marion Baxter.

109. Capeci, *Race Relations in Wartime Detroit*, 65–66.

110. Dancy, *Sand Against the Wind*, 150.

111. *Detroit Free Press*, "Owner of Sand Pit Ordered to Build Fence," July 26, 1949, 5A.

112. Dancy, *Sand Against the Wind*, 150.

113. "Frank Joyce, October 17, 2016," oral history, Detroit Historical Society.

114. *Detroit News*, "Major Q. Holley Jr., Noted Jazz Musician," October 28, 1990, 6D.

115. *Detroit Free Press*, "Great Grandson of Former Tigers Owner: Turning a Racist Legacy into One of Hope," August 22, 2017, 5A.

Conclusion

116. Metropolitan Planning Organization, Office of Planning and Environment, Federal Transportation Administration, Washington, D.C., www.transit. dot.gov/regulations-and-guidance/transportation-planning/metropolitan-planning-organization-mpo.

117. Keith Schneider, "A Case Against Sprawl," *MetroTimes*, August 18, 2004, m.metrotimes.com//Detroit/a-case-against-sprawl/content?oid=2179389.

118. Gary A. Benjamin, "Semcog's Business as Usual: A Failed Model," *Journal of Law in Society* 13, no. 1 (Fall 2011): 176.

119. Ibid., 174.

120. Ibid., 180.

121. *Report of the Option Process (T.O.P.) Task Force*, submitted to Governor William G. Milliken, February 13, 1973, 8.

122. Danny Fenster, "No Surprise: Detroit Listed as Most Segregated City in America," *Deadline Detroit*, March 26, 2014, www.deadlinedetroit. com/articles/8853/no-surprise-detroit-listed-as-most-segregated-city-in-america#w5_klt30pBTs; Kyle Vanhemart, "The Best Map Ever Made of America's Racial Segregation," *Wired*, www.wired.com/2013/08/how-segregated-is-your-city-this-eye-opening-map-shows-you.

123. Samantha Meinke, "*Milliken v. Bradley:* The Northern Battle for Desegregation," *Michigan Bar Journal* (September 2011): 22.

124. *The (Toledo) Blade*, "Tax-Base Sharing Plan Urged for Detroit Area," January 15, 1976, 1.

125. Myron Orfield, "Grand Rapids Area Metropolitics: Tax-Base Sharing in West Michigan," a report to the Grand Valley Metropolitan Council, May 1999, 1–3.

126. Hunt, "Introduction," 1–13.

127. Orfield, "Grand Rapids Area Metropolitics," 2, 4; Hunt, "Introduction," 9–13.

128. Orfield, "Grand Rapids Area Metropolitics," 5.

129. Thompson, *Whose Detroit?*, 73.

130. Ibid.

131. *New Detroit: What Has It Done?* New Detroit, Inc., 1975: 1.

132. Interview, Michael Well, June 30, 2018.

133. Cass Community Social Services, https://casscommunity.org.

134. Interview, Teresa Moon, August 15, 2018.

BIBLIOGRAPHY

Anderson, James D. *The Education of Blacks in the South, 1860–1935*. Chapel Hill: University of North Carolina Press, 1988.

Avery, Burneice. "The Eight Mile Road…Its Growth from 1920…1952." MS, Burton Historical Collection, Detroit Public Library.

———. *Walk Quietly through the Night and Cry Softly*. Detroit, MI: Balamp Publishing, 1977.

Bailey, Eric T. *African American Alternative Medicine: Using Alternative Medicine to Prevent and Control Chronic Diseases*. Santa Barbara, CA: Greenwood Press, 2012.

Bates, Beth Tompkins. "'Double V for Victory' Mobilizes Black Detroit, 1941–1946." *Freedom North: Black Freedom Struggles Outside the South, 1940–1980*. Edited by Jeanne Theoharis and Kozomi Woodard. New York: Palgrave Macmillan, 2003, 17–39.

———. *The Making of Black Detroit in the Age of Henry Ford*. Chapel Hill: University of North Carolina Press, 2012.

Berman, Lila Corwin. *Metropolitan Jews: Politics, Race, and Religion in Postwar Detroit*. Chicago: University of Chicago Press, 2015.

Borden, Ernest H. *Detroit's Paradise Valley*. Charleston, SC: Arcadia Publishing, 2003.

Boyd, Herb. *Black Detroit: A People's History of Self-Determination*. New York: Amistad/HarperCollins, 2016.

Brown, Roger. *Social Psychology*. New York: Free Press, 1965.

Capeci, Dominic J. *Race Relations in Wartime Detroit.* Philadelphia, PA: Temple University Press, 1984.

Daines, Marvel. *Be It Ever So Tumbled: The Story of a Suburban Slum.* Detroit, MI: Citizens' Housing and Planning Council of Detroit, 1920.

Dancy, John. *Sand Against the Wind.* Detroit, MI: Wayne State University Press, 1966.

Darden, Joe T., and Richard W. Thomas. *Detroit: Race Riots, Racial Conflicts, and Efforts to Bridge the Racial Divide.* East Lansing: Michigan State University Press, 2013.

Fine, Sidney. *Expanding the Frontiers of Civil Rights: Michigan, 1948–1968.* Detroit, MI: Wayne State University Press, 2000.

———. *Violence in the Model City: The Cavanagh Administration, Race Relations, and the Detroit Riot of 1967.* East Lansing: Michigan State University Press, 1989.

Freund, David M.P. *Colored Property: State Policy and White Racial Politics in Suburban America.* Chicago: University of Chicago Press, 2010.

Harding, Vincent, Robin D.G. Kelley and Earl Lewis. *We Changed the World: African Americans 1945–1970.* New York: Oxford University Press.

Harris-Slaughter, Shirley. *Our Lady of Victory: The Saga of an African American Catholic Community.* Detroit, MI: Book Khaleesi, 2004.

Hersey, John. *The Algiers Motel Incident.* New York: Bantam Books, 1968.

Hunt, Timothy L. "Introduction." In *Tax Base Sharing: Simulations for Kalamazoo County.* Kalamazoo, MI: WE. Upjohn Institute for Employment Research, 1987.

Jones, Robert K. *The Last Sleigh Ride: A Detroit Folk History.* Detroit, MI: Burning Viper Productions, 2010.

Katzman, David. *Before the Ghetto: Black Detroit in the Nineteenth Century.* Urbana: University of Illinoi Press, 1973.

Lacey, Robert. *Ford: The Men and the Machine.* Boston: Little, Brown and Company, 1986.

Levine, David Allan. *Internal Combustion: The Races in Detroit, 1915–1926.* Westport, CT: Greenwood Press, 1976.

Locke, Hubert G. *The Detroit Riot of 1967.* Detroit, MI: Wayne State University Press, 1969.

Mirel, Jeffrey. *The Rise and Fall of an Urban School System: Detroit, 1907–81.* Ann Arbor: University of Michigan Press, 1993.

Moon, Elaine Lutzman. *Untold Tales, Unsung Heroes: An Oral History of Detroit's African American Community, 1918–1967.* Detroit, MI: Wayne State University Press, 1993.

New Detroit: What Has It Done? Detroit, MI: New Detroit Inc., 1975.

Peterson, Sarah Jo. *Planning the Home Front: Building Bombers and Community at Willow Run.* Chicago: University of Chicago Press, 2013.

Seeley, Thaddeus D. *History of Oakland County Michigan.* Chicago: Lewis Publishing Company, 1912.

Sugrue, Thomas J. *The Origins of the Urban Crisis: Race and Inequality in Postwar Detroit.* Princeton, NJ: Princeton University Press, 1996.

Thompson, Heather Ann. *Whose Detroit?: Politics, Labor, and Race in a Modern American City.* Ithaca, NY: Cornell University Press, 2001.

Washington, Forrester Blanchard. *The Negro in Detroit: A Survey of the Conditions of a Negro Group in a Northern Industrial Center During the War Prosperity Period.* Detroit, MI: Associated Charities of Detroit, 1920.

Waxman, Albert. *Seekers and Creators of Community Change: An Agency's Struggle to Transform a Segregated Community During the Civil Rights Years, 1957–1963.* Lexington, KY: Creators of Community Change, 2018.

Williams, Jeremy. *Detroit: The Black Bottom Community.* Charleston, SC: Arcadia Publishing, 2009.

Wolf, Eleanor P. *Trial and Error.* Detroit, MI: Wayne State University Press, 1981.

INDEX

ABOUT THE AUTHOR

Gerald Van Dusen is professor of English at Wayne County Community College District in Detroit, Michigan. He is author of *William Starbuck Mayo*, *The Virtual Campus*, *Digital Dilemma* and *Canton Township*. His scholarly interests include American literature and culture and local history, as well as digital technology applications in higher education. A recipient of numerous awards for innovations in teaching, learning and technology, Van Dusen is a father of four and resides with Patricia, his wife of forty years, in Plymouth, Michigan.

Visit us at
www.historypress.com
....